THE
Mentoring
Year

A Step-by-Step Program for Professional Development

Susan Udelhofen
Kathy Larson

Foreword by Rick DuFour

CORWIN PRESS, INC.
A Sage Publications Company
Thousand Oaks, California

For information:

 Corwin Press, Inc.
A Sage Publications Company
2455 Teller Road
Thousand Oaks, California 91320
www.corwinpress.com

Sage Publications Ltd.
6 Bonhill Street
London EC2A 4PU
United Kingdom

Sage Publications India Pvt. Ltd.
M-32 Market
Greater Kailash I
New Delhi 110 048 India

Printed in the United States of America

Library of Congress Cataloging-in-Publication Data

Udelhofen, Susan.
The mentoring year : a step-by-step program for professional development /
by Susan Udelhofen and Kathy Larson.
          p. cm.
Includes index.
ISBN 0-7619-3925-3 (Cloth)—ISBN 0-7619-3926-1 (Paper)
1. Mentoring in education. 2. Teachers-Training of. I. Larson, Kathy.
II. Title.
LB1731.4.U34 2003
370'.71'1—dc21   2003006598

This book is printed on acid-free paper.

06 10 9 8 7 6 5 4 3

Acquisitions Editor: Jean Ward

Table of Contents

Table of Contents

DEDICATION

To my husband John, for his unconditional love and constant support and children Brian and Katie who make me proud and continually show me the true meaning of teaching and learning.

Susan Udelhofen

To my son, Jeremy, who illuminates my world with his wisdom, wit and many talents. May the strength of your spirit influence the world in peaceful and profound ways.

Kathy Larson

To the teachers who influence our children to become better citizens, with knowledge, skills and dispositions to bring peace, principles and prosperity to our world.

Susan Udelhofen and Kathy Larson

Corwin Press gratefully acknowledges the contributions of the following reviewers:

Marie Archibee, Ph.D
Supervisor, Professional Development
Department of Curriculum, Instruction and Technology
Nassau Board of Cooperative Educational Services
Massapequa Park, New York

Heidi Hayes Jacobs, Ed.D.
President, Curriculum Designs, Inc.
Adjunct Associate Professor, Teachers College, Columbia University
New York, New York

Bena Kallick, Ph.D.
Director, Technology Pathways International
Guilford, Connecticut

Dr. Joe Novak
Principal, Mill Valley High School
Shawnee, Kansas

ACKNOWLEDGMENTS

Abundant gratitude is given to the following people for their support, confidence and contributions to our work:

Rick du Four, Superintendent at Adlai Stevenson High School in Lincolnshire, Illinois , who eloquently expressed the essence of our work in the Foreword;

Mark Knicklebine, our editor and loyal servant who made two voices one;

Mary Ann Evans Patrick for "opening the door" for this project;

Jean Ward, editor of Corwin Press, for noticing the possibilities and potential of our work for building mentoring communities that focus on professional growth for all educators;

Dr. M. Robin Warden, friend and chair of the special education department at UW-Whitewater, who validated the conceptual framework of this book during many walks and talks in the woods;

Connie Salveson who used her "literary wizardry" to help us with rewriting. We are most grateful for her suggestions and most importantly her support and friendship;

Sue Grady at the Wisconsin Department of Public Instruction, for sharing her standards expertise and planting the "mentoring" seed;

Robert Garmston, from Facilitation Associates, who generously contributed to our ideas and was pleased we extended his work in this context;

Dr. Kathryn Lind at the Wisconsin Department of Public Education, who is instrumental in educational licensing reform in Wisconsin. May the flame of your passion for mentoring stay forever ignited;

Michelle Ruhe, an elementary teacher and friend, who prompted students to respond to what they thought was a good teacher and shared their wise words so we could use it in our work;

Dr. Jane Meyer, friend and teacher who believed our project was worthwhile and helped us keep the true lives of teachers at the forefront;

Dr. David Noskin, graduate school friend and teacher who arranged a visit to his high school to see real professional learning communities in action;

Carol Ross, respected teacher and lifelong friend who gave up a rainy Saturday afternoon to help identify the month-by-month realities of classroom teachers.

Prior students, for making us reflect, change and learn how to be better teachers so they could succeed;

Other friends and family, for asking about our work, encouraging us to continue in spite of barriers and inquiring when we will get our lives back!

FOREWORD

My colleague, Bob Eaker, and I have devoted a good deal of our professional lives in recent years to persuading educators that building the results-oriented, collaborative culture of a professional learning community offers the best hope for transforming schools and energizing the adults within them. One of the activities we have used on occasion to make the case for a learning community presents a scenario describing the experience of two teachers entering the profession in two different schools.

A Tale of Two Teachers

The first teacher, Beth, is assigned to teach the most difficult remedial classes in the school. Her orientation takes place on the morning before school starts, and is directed by her principal. It consists of a brief review of the faculty manual, distribution of her class list, and presentation of her keys. Most of the session deals with an explanation of how to handle specific issues, with an admonition from the principal that the new teachers must learn how to manage their own classrooms and refrain from sending their problems to the office to be solved. She struggles mightily to solve the myriad of problems that she faces as she confronts 135 apathetic students each day, and then spends three days each week and every weekend supervising the cheerleaders – one of the prerequisites for taking her job. Thrust into this sink-or-swim environment, Beth sinks, and another caring individual is lost to the teaching profession – forever.

The second teacher, Connie, has a much different experience. She is assigned a trained mentor who contacts her before the school year starts to see what questions she has about her assignment, launching a relationship that will last at least two years. Her mentor, Jim, is there every step of the way. The new teachers arrive at school a full week before the students, and Jim assists with her orientation to the school. The entire school is organized into collaborative teams based on teaching assignments, and she and Jim are assigned to the same team. He facilitates her transition onto the team and provides her with course outlines, pacing guides, rubrics, team files, common assessments, and analysis of student performance in their course for the preceding three years. He introduces her to the school's teacher evaluation system. He conducts pre-observation conferences, observes her at work in the classroom, and helps her to analyze and assess her performance based on the notes that he generated. He explains that peer coaching is valued in the school, and he asks her to observe him in the classroom and to give him feedback on some of the strategies he is using.

Jim helps Connie become familiar with the many support systems that are available to students and teachers and offers her advice as to how she can use those systems. He periodically asks her questions about her thought process in teaching the course. What does she hope students will know and be able to do as a result of today's lesson? Are prerequisite skills required to master this lesson? Do the students have those skills? How does she know? What instructional strategies will she use? How and when will she check for understanding? How will she know when students have mastered the material? What criteria will she use in judging the quality of student work? How will she respond if a student fails to accomplish the intended outcomes of the lesson or of the unit? In short, he asks her questions that help her become a reflective practitioner.

Jim was not the only person helping Connie. She had the benefit of weekly meetings, during the school day, with all the members of her course team. The entire department meets monthly. She also attended a monthly meeting of all new teachers conducted by the principal and veteran teachers. Each meeting had a theme, a reading assignment, and a required journal entry. As participants shared this experience and their thoughts over the two years of the program, they developed a kinship and provided one another with another source of ideas and comfort.

Connie also had opportunities to explore topics with colleagues through a monthly Lunch and Learn program that brought teachers together to investigate a common concern or interest. She had opportunities to earn credit on the salary schedule by enrolling in courses taught on her own campus by colleagues after school and during the summer. She participated in her team's action research project and common staff development initiative. Jim taught her how to analyze data on the performance of her students and how to identify areas where she needed help from her teammates in raising that performance. She participated in team review of model lessons taught by a member of the team and then analyzed and discussed as a group.

In a short period of time, Connie was able to identify and embrace the attitudes, expectations, beliefs, and habits that made up the unique culture of her school. She learned that, in this school, being a contributing member of a collaborative team was not optional. She learned that inquiry and reflection were part of the routine fabric of the school. She learned of the school's unrelenting focus on student learning and the tenacity with which it pursued such critical questions as, "If we truly believe all kids can learn, then what do we want them to learn, how will we know when they have learned it, and how will we respond when they don't?"

Participant Reaction

At the end of the review of this scenario, members of the audience are asked to work together in small groups to answer the following questions:

1. Was your own introduction to the profession closer to Beth's experience or Connie's experience?
2. Is it desirable to provide new teachers with a system of support similar to Connie's experience?
3. Is it feasible for schools to offer this level of support to new teachers?

The responses to these questions have been remarkably similar over the years – regardless of the grade level of the school, the age of the respondents, or where in North America I raise the question. Virtually all educators indicate that:

1. Their introduction to the profession resembled the sink-or-swim approach described in Beth's scenario. Many teachers seem to revel in the adversity and obstacles they had to overcome on their own as they began their careers.
2. It would indeed be wonderful if every teacher could have the benefit of the support and nurturing described in Connie's scenario.
3. It is not feasible that schools will offer such support any time in the near future.

At first, I was profoundly discouraged by this response. It seemed that teachers were saying, "Yes, it was hell entering this profession, and yes, it would be extremely beneficial if every new staff member had a support system as they entered the profession or became a member of a new faculty. It is unlikely, however, that schools will ever provide that support system." Even when participants were presented with examples of real schools doing everything described in Connie's scenario, participants tended to remain pessimistic about the possibility of this support becoming the rule for new staff rather than the exception.

When I probed to discover the nature of this pessimism, I found that the multiple elements of the collaborative and nurturing culture described in the scenario seemed to overwhelm the workshop participants. The specific, small, incremental steps necessary to create such a culture were obscured by the immense difference between the culture of a traditional school and the culture of a professional learning community.

My observation is that virtually no one disputes the pressing need for more effective mentoring, particularly as North America confronts a looming teacher shortage. Many states have mandated that every new teacher have the benefit of a mentor. Educators don't need to be convinced either of the dire need for or the benefits of effective mentoring; however, they would benefit from specific, practical steps regarding how they could create such programs in their schools.

This much-needed book on mentoring represents a tremendous contribution to the literature on professional learning communities, because it presents the component parts of an effective mentoring program and provides very explicit, step-by-step guidelines to build such a program in the real world of schools. The authors demonstrate great empathy for teachers and administrators who confront the challenges facing public schools. They understand the ebb and flow of a school year, and they respect the demands placed upon contemporary educators. They set out to offer ideas that are relevant and realistic – and they succeed. I also appreciate this book because it addresses the entire culture of the school, rather than limiting itself to the narrow focus of the experience of new staff. Many schools have approached mentoring as independent activity, divorced from the rest of the life of the school. They seem to forget that if a good person is placed in a bad culture, the culture will typically win. The authors understand that an effective mentoring program can reinforce the conditions that foster learning communities, but they also understand that monitoring represents just one part of the whole that comprises a learning community. The themes that resonate through their book – collaboration, reflective practice, shared vision for ongoing, job-embedded professional development, and a constant focus on student learning – must come to typify the entire school, not just the mentoring program. If new staff do not see these conditions as characteristic of their school, if they do not come to understand that these characteristics are valued in their school, they will be unlikely to embrace those characteristics, no matter how much they are encouraged in that direction by a mentor.

Thus, I recommend this book to you, not only because of the very specific tools it provides in building an effective mentoring program, but also because the authors demonstrate a deep understanding and appreciation of the fact that the qualities they call for in a model mentoring program must become the qualities that characterize the entire school. Their ideas, if put into practice, will benefit not only the newest members of a staff, but also all educators who hope to enhance their professional competence through the power of a professional learning community.

Richard P. DuFour
Superintendent of Adlai Stevenson High School, Lincolnshire, Il.
Co-author of *Professional Learning Communities at Work: Best Practices for Enhancing Student Achievement.*

ABOUT THE AUTHORS

Susan Udelhofen is an experienced classroom teacher and national staff development provider to school districts, education agencies, universities and colleges across the country. Her mentoring work focuses on developing internal learning communities that move mentoring beyond the ordinary into an extraordinary effort to improve professional practice. In addition to her mentoring work, Dr. Udelhofen provides support to several school districts that are working on issues and practices related to curriculum mapping, assessment and standards. She has taught classes in mentoring, assessment, reading, children's literature and gifted and talented education. Susan has two children and resides with her husband in Madison, Wisconsin. She can be contactedπ at sudelhof@aol.com.

Kathy Larson spent 18 years teaching middle school students and the last 10 years working exclusively in the field of professional development, concentrating her efforts on community building and continuous growth cycles for individuals, teams, and systems. Currently she is a consultant for the Cooperative Educational Service Agency #2 in Wisconsin, an adjunct faculty member at the University of Wisconsin-Whitewater, and an associate member of Consensus Associates in Terrebonne, Colorado. She has presented at national and state conferences on mentoring, has published several articles in education journals, and serves on the Wisconsin Department of Public Instruction task force to reform education licensing. Kathy lives in Whitewater, Wisconsin, and can be contacted at larson@cesa2.k12.wi.us.

Introduction

We need other people to show us, to accompany us, to hold the hope and steady our faith that we will make it. And we also need people with whom to practice: parents, friends, children, teachers. For in relationships, we both form and heal what we come again and again to name our self. This is why mentors and mentoring environments play such a key role. Without adequate support many learners . . . may decide to stay where they are.

Laurent Daloz

This book begins with our passion for teacher and student learning and our shared vision for teaching excellence. We know what it is like to begin teaching without on-going support and guidance. We understand the overwhelming feelings of uncertainty and isolation new teachers have. We experienced these challenges ourselves; yet, in spite of the obstacles, we remained in the profession because of our strong desire to teach. Statistics show that today we are the exception, not the rule.

New teachers are leaving the profession at an alarming rate. Thirty percent of beginning teachers leave the profession after the first two years; within seven years, as many as half are no longer teaching. Mentor teachers can play an important role in reversing this trend by giving new teachers the skills and role models they need to survive and thrive in the profession. Promoting the personal and professional growth and well being of new teachers greatly improves the likelihood that they will remain in the teaching profession (Stansbury & Zimmerman, 2001). A good mentoring program provides the kind of support that can reduce teacher attrition dramatically.

As mentor trainers for a number of years, we hoped and believed we were making a difference. Our mentor training primarily focused on the characteristics of good mentors, the needs of new teachers, and ways to promote reflection and collaboration. While we provided successful learning experiences for mentors, we felt our training lacked two important elements: the focus on student learning that is at the heart of all good teaching, and strategies for ongoing program support. We also wanted to ground our work in standards for good teaching as well as the latest research on effective schools.

This book presents a framework for a mentor program built on the reciprocal relationships between mentors and mentees as they create professional learning communities. This program provides a coherent learning environment for beginning teachers and those new to a grade level, building or district. It also offers a forum for our most admired teachers to pass on their accumulated wisdom about teaching practice to new generations of teachers (Darling-Hammond, 1998).

The National Board for Professional Teaching Standards (NBPTS) and the Interstate New Teacher Assessment and Support Consortium (INTASC) standards provide the guidelines for the knowledge, skills and professionalism of quality teaching reflected throughout the book. To further guide our research, we looked to Peter Senge's *Schools That Learn,* Robert Garmston's *The Adaptive School*, Rick DuFour's *Professional Learning Communities at Work,* and Tom Guskey's *Evaluating Professional Development*. Building on their ideas we structured a mentor program consisting of four themes that are embedded throughout our book.

- Collaboration
- Reflective practice
- Shared vision for professional growth
- Student learning

These guiding principles provide the framework within which mentors and mentees can develop partnerships in a professional learning community.

Collaboration

> *If I want to teach well, it is essential that I explore my inner terrain. But I can get lost in there, practicing self-delusion and running in self-serving circles. So I need the guidance that a community of collegial discourse provides – to say nothing of the support such a community can offer to sustain me in the trials of teaching and the cumulative and collective wisdom about this craft that can be found in every faculty worth its salt.*
>
> *Parker Palmer*

Meaningful collaboration doesn't just happen as a result of suggestion or chance. It is an ongoing process that needs to be structured, planned, and learned. There must be many opportunities for mentors and mentees to share ideas, perspectives, and expertise about teaching and learning. Teachers must work together as collaborators and colleagues to better understand both their own school experience and that of their students. This type of collaboration changes the mentor/mentee relationship from a hierarchical relationship to a reciprocal relationship based on mutual respect and learning. This effort combines the abilities and energies of beginning teachers with the experience of veteran teachers, and enables both to simultaneously contribute to the process of improved learning for teachers and students (Middleton, 2000). The activities presented in this book encourage mentors and mentees to collaborate as they explore issues related to learning. Whether they are completed independently, in mentor/mentee pairs, or in small groups, all activities promote a spirit of mutual sharing and collegiality.

Reflective Practice

[Reflection] emancipates us from merely impulsive and merely routine activity.
Put in positive terms, thinking enables us to direct our activities with foresight
and to plan according to ends-in-view, or purposes of which we are aware. It
enables us to act in deliberate and intentional fashion to attain future objects or
to come into command of what is now distant and lacking.

John Dewey

Thoughtful, reflective dialogue helps us see each other's point of view, become sensitive to each other's strengths and weaknesses, and act in each other's best interests. In practice, however, reflection can be difficult to integrate into our daily teaching routine in a sustained, meaningful way. We believe that if we want teachers to reflect, we must offer them a wide range of ongoing opportunities to think and talk about their teaching practice. The mentoring program we outline in this book provides ample occasion for mentor and mentee to practice the art of reflection and develop a culture of reflective thought.

Even when conditions are conducive for reflective dialogue, it can be difficult for teachers to think and talk openly about their work in meaningful ways. For the most part, teachers function in the isolation of their classrooms with little opportunity or encouragement to engage in any type of reflective activity with other educators. Even when opportunities to reflect on practice are presented and supported, many teachers have little understanding of what reflection really means and how it is accomplished. To help with this process, we include structured activities that involve posing questions and teaching dilemmas, discussing possible solutions or procedures, implementing strategies, analyzing student work products, and evaluating results in a collaborative manner.

Shared Vision for Professional Growth

Mentors can guide a mentee's sense of the possible.
The mentor's vision inspires and informs. Sharing stories, modeling behaviors
and holding up a mirror empower the mentee. By fostering continuous
reflection and assessing learning outcomes, movement is encouraging during
and after completion of the relationship.

Lois Zachary

A solid mentoring program presents opportunities for mentors and mentees to explore their value and belief systems in order to create the best possible learning environment for students. As Nancy Hoffman observes in *Schools That Learn* (2000), "When teachers begin their careers it is based on something to be gotten or had rather than something engaged, constructed and connected to the participants. These practices shape the beginning teacher's identity as one who implements rather than produces knowledge."

A mentoring program must provide opportunities for teachers to construct their own teaching identity, a vision based on teaching standards and research, as well as on their own experiences and reflection and those of other teachers. As teachers engage in meaningful conversations about teaching and learning, work through teaching dilemmas and think deeply about challenging educational issues in a safe environment, a beginning teacher's identity begins to emerge. In this environment, new ideas can be explored and teaching practices can be examined without fear of recrimination. The activities presented in this book provide many opportunities for self-reflection, group reflection, and analysis of one's own beliefs, history and practice.

Student Learning

> *The focus of traditional schools is teaching; the focus of the professional learning community is student learning. The difference is much more than semantics. It represents a fundamental shift in the teacher-student relationship. This new relationship would not allow for the familiar teacher lament, "I taught it – they just did not learn it."*
>
> Rick DuFour

A mentoring program must not lose touch with the real purpose of teaching: keeping students at the center of our practice. Professional growth leads to better teaching and, ultimately, to improved student learning. The activities in this book provide opportunities to use real student data and feedback for meaningful discussion after methods and activities are implemented in the classroom. This guided, interactive dialogue will address teaching standards and methods, student characteristics and learning styles, curriculum, and assessment. Participants will examine their own student learning history, explore assessment strategies, investigate curriculum issues, analyze national, state and local standards, and consider various teaching methods – all focused on the goal of fostering student learning.

ORGANIZATION OF THE BOOK

This book is designed to guide both mentees and mentors through a cycle of learning based on teaching standards. The mentors and mentees will collect information, discuss teaching experiences in a variety of settings, apply what they have learned, and assess the outcomes. This cycle focuses on what is at the heart of good teaching by emphasizing and modeling teacher and student learning. Understanding the time constraints experienced by teachers, we knew it would be important to create a book that is easy to use. To that end, we've laid out a step-by-step process that calls for one two-hour mentor/mentee gathering each month, along with informal mentor/mentee interactions throughout the month. For each month of either a nine-month or year-round school program, we present a set of desired outcomes grounded in teaching standards, followed by a repertoire of ready-to-use activities that promote collaboration and reflection. Each month builds on the previous month's focus and activities. A central focus of the program is a *Weekly Teacher Reflection Journal* that helps teachers collect information and observations related to their classroom practice as well as each month's specific topic. At the end of the cycle the learning partners will analyze the information they have collected in order to set meaningful goals as part of an ongoing professional development plan.

The monthly format includes the following components:

- **Overview or Focus of the Chapter**
  Each chapter begins with a brief discussion of the focus for this month's mentee/mentor work.
- **Learning Targets**
  The learning objectives of each of the suggested activities are outlined at the beginning of each chapter.
- **Resources**
  We include a list of resources that can be used to enhance and enrich the presented activities. This is especially useful for future reference.
- **Activities**
  Each chapter includes activities that assist mentors and mentees in collaborating and reflecting on a given topic. Each activity is accompanied with an overview, suggestions for implementation, and a time estimate.
- **Required Forms Section**
  Forms that are to be completed each month can be found in the required forms section at the end of each month's activities. This section includes the *Monthly Seminar Planning Form*, the *Weekly Teacher Reflection Journal Form*, the *Monthly Reflection Journal Summary Form,* and the *Monthly Support Seminar Evaluation Form.*

MONTHLY SUPPORT SEMINARS

The theme for each month is reflected in the agenda for the monthly support seminars. Here all participants gather to discuss their observations and share the learning process as colleagues. The following is an overview of the topics addressed throughout the year.

MONTH ONE: Introducing the Mentoring Partners to the Reflective Process

We begin with activities and tools designed to assist the mentee and mentor to get to know each other. The framework of the mentor program is described, and a timeline is established for both weekly meetings and monthly support seminars. The *Weekly Teacher Reflection Journal* and *Monthly Reflection Journal Summary* are introduced and will be the focus of reflection and dialogue throughout the mentor/mentee relationship. Mentors and mentees begin the process of paired learning using the *Norms of Collaboration* (Garmston, 1999). The norms describe the approach mentors and mentees will use to discuss and analyze each other's teaching performance in the following months.

MONTH TWO: Exploring Our Current Reality

The activities in Month Two are designed to help participants gather information about the school, district and the community. The mentor and mentee assess their learning needs and complete a plan to meet those needs in the coming months.

MONTH THREE: Analyzing Professional Practice

The mentoring partners discuss the knowledge, skills and professional standards represented in the National Board of Professional Teaching Standards (NBPTS). Through dialogue and reflection about the teaching standards, the partners will create a "big picture" survey of their own professional practice. The activities focus on collecting examples, resources, and other useful information that demonstrate how quality teaching standards are represented in their school and classrooms. The *Weekly Teacher Reflection Journal* for this month will focus on the partners' reflections on how the standards are applied in their everyday teaching, and the effect of quality teaching on student learning.

MONTH FOUR: Analyzing Classroom Environment

This month's activities are centered on how each teacher's classroom environment is structured to meet diverse student needs and to maximize learning. The effect of various classroom environments on student learning is explored through reading, classroom observation and teacher interviews. Participants record their explorations in the *Weekly Teacher Reflection Journal* and discuss them during the partners' meeting. The partners then discuss how they are currently structuring their classroom environment and how students are reacting to it. They compare this to the best practices reflected in the professional teaching standards and note further changes that would help students learn more effectively in their own classroom.

MONTH FIVE: Understanding Assessment

This month's activities will help teachers gain a better understanding of assessment and explore their own assessment experiences. Various assessment strategies will be introduced. The learning partners will analyze student work, discuss issues related to grading, create an assessment plan and participate in a type of performance assessment. Each activity is designed to promote reflective thought and discussion of the complexities of meaningful student assessment. The *Weekly Teacher Reflection Journal* will focus on the effectiveness of current assessment practices and how assessment relates to student learning and achievement.

MONTH SIX: Content Standards and Curriculum

In Month Six, the partners will analyze the content of teaching and learning. Collaborative activities will promote discussion of curriculum and academic standards for teaching. Partners will explore their current curriculum and determine what additional curriculum information is needed for effective teaching. They will also analyze national, state and local academic standards and examine the connection between curriculum and standards. The *Weekly Teacher Reflection Journal* will focus on this analysis.

MONTH SEVEN: Instructional Methods

Teaching is more than a series of activities. It must include instructional strategies based on curriculum, standards, and student needs; these instructional strategies are the focus of Month Seven. Partners will analyze student behavior, participate in classroom visits, examine how various teaching methods meet the needs of a diverse student population, and develop learning goals based on current practice. The *Weekly Teacher Reflection Journal* will focus on teaching methods, instructional strategies and documentation related to the classroom visits.

MONTH EIGHT: Setting Goals

This month, partners will analyze the data collected as a result of the activities throughout the first six months, including all *Monthly Reflection Journal Summary* forms and other artifacts collected throughout the year. By responding to such statements as "What I most need help with is…" and "What I most need to work on in my practice is…," partners will set measurable learning goals that lead to professional growth and maximized student learning outcomes.

MONTH NINE: Writing the Professional Development Plan

In Month Nine, partners will create a professional development plan based on the learning goals set the previous month. Goals, a plan of action, and a timeline are the essential components of the professional development plan. Both mentor and mentee will collaborate on the plan; optionally, the mentor may complete a plan as well as the mentee.

MONTH TEN AND BEYOND: The Cycle Continues: Sustaining the Momentum

The final section explores next steps to continue the collaboration and support as the professional development plan is implemented. Suggestions for future work that addresses the ongoing needs of mentor and mentee to continue the learning partnership are addressed.

TOOLS AND CHECKLISTS: Appendix

This section includes tools and monthly checklists to assist all mentees, mentors, administrators, and program coordinators to implement the mentor program. The tools and checklists include:

- Monthly checklists outlining key classroom and district responsibilities for mentors and mentees, as well as school occurrences throughout the year that can affect teaching and student learning;
- Monthly administrator duties that are necessary to support and encourage the mentor program;
- The monthly organization and implementation responsibilities of the mentor program coordinator.

CONCLUSION

Readers who are familiar with the requirements for National Board teacher certification will recognize the linkages to our mentoring program. Just as we have integrated NBPTS standards as expressions of quality teaching, many of our activities consist of documenting evidence of how those standards are actualized in the classroom. This practice of collecting documentary evidence of standards in practice is an important part of attaining National Board Certification – and a part that many teachers struggle with. Educators who wish to apply for certification will find this program an excellent way to prepare.

Our mentoring program, then, seeks to achieve more than creating a nurturing environment for new teachers, as important as that objective is. Ideally, the program we outline becomes a way for the entire faculty to gain a practical familiarity with the highest standards of the teaching profession, and to prepare to gain recognition for mastering these standards. Our program seeks ultimately to create a community of educators who learn from their practice and who share their insights with their colleagues as they create an ever-improving, ever-renewing learning environment for children.

RESOURCES

Daloz, Laurent (1999). *Mentor: Guiding the journey of adult learners.* San Francisco, CA: Jossey-Bass.

Darling-Hammond, Linda (1998). Teacher learning that supports student learning. *Educational Leadership,* 55(5), 6-11.

Dewey, John (1904/64). Why reflective thinking must be an educational aim. In *John Dewey on Education,* ed. R.D. Archambault, 313-38. Chicago: The University of Chicago Press.

DuFour, Rick & Eaker, Robert (1998). *Professional learning communities at work: Best practices for enhancing student achievement.* Alexandria: VA: Association for Supervision and Curriculum Development.

Garmston, Robert, Wellman, Bruce. (1999). *The adaptive school: A sourcebook for developing collaborative groups.* Norwood MA: Christopher-Gordon.

Guskey, Thomas (2000). *Evaluating professional development.* Thousand Oaks CA: Corwin Press

Hoffman, Nancy (2000). Learning to teach. In *Schools That Learn*, ed. P. Senge, 406-8. New York: Doubleday.

Middleton, Valerie (2000). A community of learners. *Educational Leadership,* 57 (8) 51-53.

National Staff Development Council. (2001). *Tools for growing the NSDC standards.* Oxford, OH: National Staff Development Council.

Palmer, P. (1990). *The active life.* San Francisco, CA: Jossey-Bass.

Richardson, J. (August/September, 2001). Learning teams: When teachers work together, knowledge and rapport grow. *Tools for Schools*. Oxford, OH: National Staff Development Council.

Richardson, J. (August/September, 2002). Think outside the clock: Create time for professional learning. *Tools for Schools*. Oxford, OH: National Staff Development Council.

Senge, Peter, (2000). *Schools that learn.* New York: Doubleday.

Stansbury, Kendyll & Zimmerman, Joy (2001). Lifelines to the Classroom: Designing support for beginning teachers. *West Ed. Knowledge Brief.* San Francisco CA: West Ed

An Overview

THE MENTORING YEAR: AN OVERVIEW

This book presents a model for a teacher mentoring program that promotes individual, paired, and small group learning in order to create a collaborative, professional learning community. The structure of this mentor program strongly encourages a team-building approach in which both mentee and mentor complete designated tasks as they work together to improve student learning.

Both mentoring partners keep reflection journals to record weekly entries and monthly summaries, meet weekly, and attend monthly support seminars where all mentees and mentors gather for joint activities that focus on specific topics. The monthly support seminars provide a designated time for mentees and mentors to interact with other teachers who are new to the profession, those new to the grade level, building or district, and other mentors, in the spirit of collegiality and shared learning. We ask the learning partners to think about each month's experience, to analyze how and what they learned affected their own teaching, to discuss the highs and lows of the month's experience, and to look for emerging patterns, themes, strengths, and growing concerns. This reflective thinking, together with the suggested activities, results in products, information, and observations that partners collect and use to set goals and create a professional development plan for future work. At the end of each support seminar, participants complete an evaluation of the program. We understand that the mentor/mentee partnership may not always be an ideal match. This difficulty can be eased by providing regular opportunities for participants to interact with many supportive teachers in a seminar setting.

In the following section we share an overview of the essential components of a mentor program based on what we have learned from our mentor training experience and provide a *suggested* design structure for this mentor program. We believe that the structure is one that many schools will find useful; however, we recognize that each school and district has its own unique culture, climate, resources, and people. Therefore, we encourage you to take the ideas we present and modify them to best fit your needs.

Mentor Program Components

Teacher Reflection Journals

Participants are required to keep a *Weekly Teacher Reflection Journal* to record their reflections each week. These journals are used throughout the program as the basis of discussions between the mentoring partners, and as a way to focus their attention on the critical elements of teaching and student learning. Excerpts from the journals can be discussed during the weekly mentor/mentee meetings as well as during the monthly support seminars. This important resource is the foundation for the mentoring relationship and is a crucial component of this program.

Participants are also asked to review and summarize their weekly journal entries each month, using the *Monthly Reflection Journal Summary* form. This summary process helps the partners detect emerging patterns, themes, and concerns that arise from their weekly reflections. Teachers save the forms and use them to develop professional development goals based on their observed strengths and needs. More information about the *Weekly Teacher Reflection Journal* and the *Monthly Reflection Journal Summary* is included in Month One.

Weekly Mentee/Mentor Meetings

It is crucial that the mentoring partners meet weekly. We suggest that the mentor and mentee agree on an established time to meet each week – say, each Wednesday morning from 7:15 to 7:45, for instance. The next section outlines a number of strategies to establish this meeting schedule. During these meetings, the partners may discuss teaching dilemmas, successes, excerpts from the *Weekly Teacher Reflection Journal,* and the topic of the upcoming monthly support seminar.

Monthly Support Seminars

The monthly support seminars are designed to provide opportunities for mentors and mentees to participate in activities that address specific topics based on teaching standards. The book offers a repertoire of activities for participants to choose from and a variety of ways to implement them. There are activities suitable for individuals to complete on their own, with their partners, or in small groups. Each monthly chapter includes a list of the activities, along with the purpose, the participants and required time for each. This format enables the partners to preview the list, decide which activities each would like to focus on at that particular support seminar, and then complete a feedback form to communicate their choices to the mentor program coordinator (we'll discuss this important position in the next section). The coordinator sets the agenda based on the feedback of the participants. It is not necessary for all participants to engage in the same activity. A sample feedback form and a suggested agenda for the support seminars are included on the following pages.

SUGGESTED MONTHLY SEMINAR PLANNING FORM

MONTHLY SEMINAR PLANNING FORM

Date _____

Mentor Name _____

Mentee Name _____

Monthly Seminar Topic _____

I have reviewed this month's suggested activities and would like to focus on the following partner or small group activity:

Activity Number _____

Title _____

Mentee or Mentor Name _____

SUGGESTED MONTHLY SEMINAR AGENDA

Introductions This may only be necessary for the first monthly support seminar. After month one this time can be allocated to the monthly topic.	10 minutes
Monthly Reflection Journal Summary Opportunity to self-select groups to discuss the teaching dilemmas, events, successes, etc., based on the *Monthly Reflection Journal Summary*. The coordinator may decide how the groups are formed, or they can be randomly organized. *Be aware that self-selecting groups can use up valuable time.*	25 minutes
Monthly Topic Each participant chooses an activity to work on. Groups are formed based on the choices of the mentors and mentees. Mentors and mentees must review the activities prior to coming to the seminar. If materials are needed to complete the activity, participants should bring the necessary materials with them.	70 minutes
Wrap-up, Evaluations and Plans for Next Month	15 minutes

In most months, it will not be possible to complete all of the activities we present during the monthly seminar. Therefore, we encourage mentees and mentors to complete additional activities of interest independently now or at a later date. At the end of the cycle, when the mentee and mentor have created learning goals and professional development plans, they may decide to return to specific sections and complete additional activities.

MONTHLY SUPPORT SEMINAR EVALUATION

Participants should complete an evaluation of the support seminars each month. This feedback allows the coordinator, administrators, mentors and mentees to gauge the effectiveness of the mentor program, identify difficulties and successes, and to make continual improvements as the year progresses. You may wish to consider an evaluation format like this one:

MONTHLY SUPPORT SEMINAR EVALUATION MONTH/TOPIC:
1. List the activity you chose to focus on this month:
2. List the learning partner(s) you worked with to complete this activity:
3. What was the most important thing you learned about this month's topic?
4. How has this month's activity influenced your classroom teaching?
5. What other monthly activities included in this chapter do you plan to complete?
6. What data will you collect as a result of this month's activity?
7. What suggestions do you have for improving the monthly seminars?

Nurturing an Effective Mentoring Program

Successful mentoring relationships are more likely to happen in the context of a supportive school environment that provides leadership, structure, resources and time. While most of this book focuses on the activities of the mentor and mentee, a solid mentoring program must also become a highly visible and integral part of the academic and administrative culture of the school. To provide this type of learning environment, we suggest the following components be included or addressed before you begin.

Recruiting Mentors

Recruiting experienced teachers to serve as mentors will be one of the most crucial initial steps in the program. Some schools will be fortunate to recruit a sufficient number of mentors to provide partners for all new teachers. The fine points of selecting the most qualified mentors or making the proper match with each new faculty member may have to wait until the program is more established. Nonetheless, it is important for mentor program administrators to consider the characteristics of effective mentors as well as strategies for pairing mentors and mentees.

Successful mentors share a number of common characteristics:

Trustworthy

The mentor must be able to serve as confidant, anchor and source of support to the new teacher. The trust between the mentor and mentee creates an atmosphere in which the partners feel free to ask for help, expose insecurities, take risks, and celebrate successes. It allows both mentor and mentee to discuss, accept, and work through teaching dilemmas with the ultimate shared goal of improving learning experiences for students.

Effective Communicator

Good communication skills are crucial for creating an open, honest relationship between the learning partners. The mentor must be able to listen, ask the right questions, and be open to feedback.

Competent and Responsible

A central role of the mentor is to model the traits of effective teachers to new faculty members. These traits include knowledge of and commitment to the teaching profession, integrity, professionalism and teaching competence. More than merely senior faculty members, mentors should be excellent teachers.

Good Interpersonal Skills

Most mentees need a mentor who will nurture and guide them along the path to becoming an effective teacher. To fulfill this role the mentor needs to be approachable, positive, caring, and understanding.

Collaborator

It is important that the mentor teacher be open to sharing ideas and expertise, solving problems, and working as a member of a team in the spirit of collegiality to develop a true learning community.

Matching Mentors and Mentees

What are the best criteria for deciding which mentor to pair with which mentee? Is it best to pair teachers in the same grade level, content area or building? Or is it more advantageous to pair teachers whose personality traits seem more compatible? There is no one answer that will work for every pairing; we've seen successes and problems associated with both arrangements. For some, it is beneficial to be paired with a teacher who is nurturing and will provide the type of support that crosses all content areas, grade levels and physical location. For others, a nurturing relationship isn't as important as the grade level or content area expertise and knowledge a mentor with a similar teaching assignment can provide. To further complicate matters, many districts are experiencing a shortage of qualified mentors that limits the pairing possibilities. We believe it is best to receive input and guidance from both mentors and those who are organizing the program to decide what works best given the culture and characteristics of your school and district.

What if a teacher isn't matched to a mentor who serves his or her needs well? Reassignment may be a luxury that the likely shortage of mentors does not afford. One of the benefits of our program structure, which combines both one-on-one and group experiences, is that participants have many opportunities to interact with a variety of teachers. This interaction can help to alleviate some matching complications. Beyond that, however, one of the central goals of the program is to help all participants develop their abilities to work together as colleagues, taking each others' personalities and communication styles into account as they pursue common learning goals.

Mentor Program Coordinator

It is important to assign a program coordinator to oversee the organization of the monthly meetings and to keep mentors and mentees informed about dates, times, locations, agendas and necessary supplies. The coordinator also facilitates communication among the mentors and mentees to determine specific topics for the focus of that particular month's support seminar.

In most cases the coordinator is a curriculum leader or resource teacher who is appointed by the principal or superintendent. We recommend that the coordinator have good organizational skills as well as some knowledge about mentoring and teaching standards. It is possible that the participating teachers might share some of the responsibilities, but one person should be appointed to oversee the process. In our experience, if there is not a person "in charge" there is a greater likelihood that the monthly support meetings will not happen. We include a list of coordinator responsibilities by month in the Appendix.

Administrative Support

Establishing, implementing, and sustaining a sound mentor program requires on-going support from district leadership. The superintendent and building principal play key roles in providing the necessary guidance, acknowledgment and reinforcement to all teachers involved in the mentor program. These support strategies include participating in the monthly support seminars, providing the necessary materials and information about the district as needed, modifying mentor and mentee schedules, and promoting the program to all faculty, parents and community. In the Appendix, we offer monthly checklists and strategies for administrative support and involvement.

Teacher Union Support

Another important stakeholder is the local teacher union. Gaining union support may require that the school or district make a number of assurances regarding the mentor program. The teachers' union will want to know that the program is not intended in any way to erode the administration's responsibility to supervise teachers. It is also important to provide reassurance that the communication between mentors and their learning partners is confidential and that mentors will never be expected to give incriminating information in any disciplinary actions that might arise against the new teacher. The union may also want to know if mentors or their learning partners will receive additional compensation for the extra meetings and work involved. Most importantly, the union should be assured that the program shares the union's goals of supporting new teachers, building strong learning communities within the school and the district, and helping teachers new to the system become informed, skilled and caring professionals.

Finding the Time

We suggest that the mentor/mentee pair meet informally for 20 to 30 minutes each week to discuss issues that arise from their daily teaching experience. They can also use this time to discuss the topic of the monthly seminar and review the activities for that month. In addition, two hours should be allocated for monthly support seminars for all mentors and mentees. It works best when a set day and time are established for the monthly seminars. For example, the coordinator might designate the second Tuesday of the month from 3:45 to 5:45 for the support seminars.

Teachers have incredibly busy schedules; the challenge of finding the time to meet on a regular basis is daunting. We posed that concern to a group of our teacher colleagues and asked them to offer suggestions as to where they could "find the time." Here are some of their ideas:

Informal ways for mentors and mentees to schedule 20-30 minutes per week:

- Creative scheduling
  - Common prep time
  - Parallel scheduling – all students going to specials at the same time
- Sharing students – combining two or more classes for a joint activity, thereby freeing up time for mentor and mentee to meet
- Teaching assistants or parent volunteers can supervise non-instructional activities
  - Extended lunchtime
  - Videos
  - Field trips
- Hiring floating substitute teachers to free teachers in 30-minute blocks of time
- Early morning meetings (for instance, breakfast each Friday morning)
- After school
- Lunch time (partners might get together for lunch every Wednesday, for example)
- Mentors and mentees are released from non-instructional duties, such as early morning supervision or recess duty
- Principal, assistant principal, or curriculum director take over class supervision

Formal strategies to plan monthly support seminars:

- Banking time – extend the school day by 5-10 minutes per day to enable extra staff development days
- Adjust start and end time
  - Late starts
  - Early dismissals
- Use existing staff development days
- Staff meetings
- School assemblies – when all teachers do not need to attend

SUGGESTED TIME COMMITMENT

Who	What	Time	Total Time
Mentor/Mentee	Weekly meetings/classroom visits	30 minutes per week	5-6 hours per month
	Teacher Reflection Journal	20 – 30 minutes per week	
	Monthly support seminars	2 hours per month	
Coordinator	Planning time	2 hours per month	4 hours per month
	Monthly support seminars	2 hours per month	
Administrator	30 minutes per week to free mentors/mentees to meet	2 hours per month	4 hours per month
	Monthly support seminars	2 hours per month	

Compensation

There are many ways that mentees and mentors can be compensated for their time. Some districts offer stipends or extended contract time for mentees and mentors; others credit mentoring time to professional development or recertification hours, or join efforts with the local college or university to offer the monthly seminars as part of a for-credit course.

CONCLUSION

The mentoring program we outline here is designed as a guide to get you started. As you gain more experience, you will be able to modify it to meet the unique needs of your district. Adopt the methods and activities that work for you; amend or skip those that don't. The core elements of our program include a commitment to a regular meeting schedule, a focus on standards of quality teaching, the use of the teacher reflection journals, and the goal of creating a collaborative, collegial learning environment. The details may be rearranged to suit your situation. What is important is not strict adherence to these suggestions, but that you strive to implement a program that supports mentoring relationships and builds a professional learning community.

Month One

INTRODUCING THE MENTORING PARTNERS
TO THE REFLECTIVE PROCESS

With an attitude of unassuming modesty
You offer no danger or threat to those around you.
Sincere modesty invites loyal alignment with others.
Do not boast and glare overtly.
Keep the jade and treasures subtly reserved within the bosom.
A posture of a humble heart and genuine respect for the wise
Will bring blessings from all directions.
    Huang & Lynch,
    Mentoring:
    The Tao of Giving
    and Receiving Wisdom

INTRODUCTION TO MONTH ONE

The goal for the first month of this mentoring program is to start both the mentor and mentee on the path of developing a collegial relationship directly focused on the critical elements of teaching and student learning. When the mentoring experience is conscientiously grounded in teacher and student learning, the mentoring relationship is much more likely to become a satisfactory learning experience for both partners (Zachary, 2000). Instead of being mentor-driven, with the mentor taking full responsibility for the mentee's learning, the mentee plays a more self-directed role, as both partners share responsibility for the learning priorities, setting, and resources. As the learning team evolves, the mentoring partners also share accountability for achieving goals for professional development.

Dialogue and discussion are the primary skills of the mentoring partnership. This chapter introduces the *Norms of Collaboration* (Garmston, 1999) as the style of communication between the learning partners, so that each may benefit from future dialogue, reflection, and action. These guidelines for productive teamwork prepare the partners to maximize the quality of their learning as they begin to analyze their professional performance related to the National Board of Professional Teaching Standards in Month Three.

After learning about the norms and their definitions, the partners begin to apply these practices through a series of get-acquainted exercises. The Norms of Collaboration Inventory (see Activity1-1) is a self-assessment tool teachers can use to rate their own use of these collaborative discussion techniques.

Weekly Journal and Monthly Summary

The *Weekly Teacher Reflection Journal* (adapted from Brookfield, 1987) is the foundation for reflection in the mentoring partnership. It is the only required activity to be completed every week throughout the nine-month program. Each partner is responsible for duplicating the *Weekly Teacher Reflection Journal* sheets (found in the Required Forms Section of Months One through Nine), completing them at the end of the week, and saving them. In Months One and Two, the partners will use the same reflection questions. The journal pages become more specific in Months Three through Seven, as questions are added or revised to reflect the focus of each month's activities.

The *Monthly Reflection Journal Summary* activity is also required each month, and is used at the mentor/mentee monthly meetings. Prior to each month's seminar, partners individually summarize their weekly reflections using the form provided. These summaries help the partners observe patterns and themes within both their teaching and the responses of their students. Participants must save the summary sheets each month and use them to complete the goal setting and planning activities in Months Eight and Nine.

Through this process of weekly reflection and monthly summaries, the partners each build a portfolio of their explorations, observations, and analysis of their teaching experiences. This treasure trove of thoughts and ideas provides fuel for the dialogue between the partners, and becomes the raw material from which each will formulate their professional growth plans.

Other Activities

The partners may choose to complete any of the remaining Month One activities that your time and interests permit. Activity 1-2 is an inventory that encourages introspection about the individual's perception as a teacher. The discussion between partners is also a forum for practicing the Norms of Collaboration. The norms worksheet (Activity worksheet 1-1) can be filled out independently or with your partner after completing Activity 1-2. Activity 1-3 asks the partners to reflect on teachers they've had in the past who may serve as role models in their personal and professional lives, and to consider the kind of role models they would like to be for their own students. Once again, the norms inventory can be used before or after this activity. The sentence stems in Activity 1-4 allow partners to get acquainted and to practice the norms in the context of the discussion.

LEARNING TARGETS

- Respect each other as collaborative partners in education.

- Practice collaborative skills using the Norms of Collaboration as the communication for professional growth.

- Use the *Weekly Teacher Reflection Journal* as the focus of reflection and insights from this month's activities.

- Analyze the month's reflections and summarize them in writing on the *Monthly Reflection Journal Summary* worksheet.

RESOURCES

Barth, R. S. (2001). *Learning by heart*. San Francisco: Jossey-Bass.

Brookfield, S. D. (1995). *Becoming a critically reflective teacher.* San Francisco: Jossey-Bass.

Cooper, C., & Boyd, J. (1994). *Collaborative approaches to professional learning and reflection.* Tasmania, Australia: Global Learning Communities.

Dantonio, M. (1995). *Collegial coaching: Inquiry into the teaching self.* Bloomington, IN: Phi Delta Kappa.

Denmark, V. M. & Podsen, I. J. (2000). The mettle of a mentor. *Journal of Staff Development, 21.* 18-22.

Distad, L. S., Chase, B., Germundsen, R., & Brownstein, J. C. (2000). Putting their heads together. *Journal of Staff Development, 21.* 49 – 51.

Garmston, R. J. & Wellman, B. M. (1999). *The adaptive school.* Norwood, MA: Christopher-Gordon Publishers, Inc.

Lipton, L. & Wellman, B. (2001). *Mentoring matters: A practical guide to learning-focused relationships.* Sherman, CT: Mira Via.

Patterson, K., Grenny, J., McMillan, R., & Switzler, A. (2002). *Crucial conversations: Tools for talking when stakes are high.* New York: McGraw-Hill.

Russell. T. & Munby, H. (1992). *Teachers and teaching: From classroom to reflection.* Bristol, PA: Falmer Press.

Senge, P. (2000). *Schools that learn.* New York: Doubleday.

Zachary, L. J. (2000). *The mentor's guide.* San Francisco: Jossey-Bass.

Zeichner, K., Klehr, M., & Caro-Bruce, C. (2000). Pulling their own levers. *Journal of Staff Development, 21.* 36-39.

MONTH ONE SUPPORT SEMINAR ACTIVITIES

Number	Activity	Completed Date
	REQUIRED ACTIVITIES • Monthly Seminar Planning Form • Weekly Teacher Reflection Journal • Monthly Reflection Journal Summary • Monthly Support Seminar Evaluation	
1-1	**Norms of Collaboration** (REQUIRED THIS MONTH ONLY) **Purpose:** To introduce collaborative communication strategies that guide future discussion and meetings **Materials:** Activity worksheet 1-1, pen/pencil **Who:** Mentor and/or Mentee and/or seminar participants **Time:** 20 minutes to individually read and self-assess; 5-10 minutes to discuss	
1-2	**Reflection Inventory** **Purpose:** To get acquainted using the prompts and practicing the Norms of Collaboration. **Materials:** Activity worksheet 1-2, Activity worksheet 1-1, pen/pencil **Who:** Mentor and Mentee **Time:** 45 min. – 1 hr.	
1-3	**Role Model Profile** **Purpose:** To discuss prior experiences that influence the partners' views of teaching. **Materials:** Activity worksheet 1-3, Activity worksheet 1-1, pen/pencil **Who:** Mentor & Mentee **Time:** 30 min.	
1-4	**Partner Interview** **Purpose:** To introduce the partners and allow them to practice the Norms of Collaboration **Materials:** Activity worksheet 1-4, Activity worksheet 1-1, pen/pencil **Who:** Mentor & Mentee **Time:** 30 – 45 min.	

ACTIVITY 1-1

THE SEVEN NORMS OF COLLABORATION

INTRODUCTION: A skill is something that someone knows how to do. A skill becomes a norm when it is "normal" behavior in the group. *The Seven Norms of Collaboration* are constructed from a cognitive coaching model (Costa & Garmston, 1994) for the purpose of creating and sustaining effective working relationships for collective growth. Each norm is deceptively simple, yet requires continued application and refinement to become a normal part of professional communication. Individuals and groups select goals from the seven norms to practice and monitor. Later, they reflect on the how the norms affect the collaborative process for themselves and for the group.

DIRECTIONS: Read each of the descriptions and use the inventory on the next page to assess your use of the skills. Then establish goals for improving your use of the norms, either individually or with your partner. Use the skills to practice, monitor, and reflect upon your goals as you proceed through the activities.

1. **Pause:** It takes from three to five seconds for most people to process high level thoughts; therefore, pausing is essential for critical thinking. Here are some examples:
   - The speaker allows time for thought after a question or response
   - Respondents pause before responding to a question or comment
   - Individuals take time to allow ideas and questions to settle in and to reflect on what they have heard.

2. **Paraphrase:** A well-crafted paraphrase sends the message, "I am trying to understand you – and, therefore, I value what you have to say." To paraphrase effectively, listen carefully and observe both the content and emotions of the speaker. Signal your intention to paraphrase by using a reflective stem. Some examples of reflective stems:
   - *You're suggesting...*
   - *You're proposing...*
   - *So, you are thinking that...*
   - *So, what you're wondering is...*
   - *You're pondering the effects of...*
   - *Your hunch is that...*

3. **Probe for specificity:** To identify generalizations, deletions, and distortions, gently probe for specificity when you hear:
   - Vague nouns and pronouns such as "they."
   - Subjective words such as "improve", "unmotivated", "disrupting", or "hyperactive."
   - Comparators such as "best", "slower", etc. Ask for the criteria used to make the comparison.
   - Rule words: "You shouldn't"; "We have to". Probe for the rules behind such statements; ask, "Where is it written?"

4. **Put ideas on the table:** Groups work productively when their members put forward ideas that are supported by data, both qualitative and quantitative. Observations about student learning, school climate, teacher satisfaction, parental attitudes, and the like, are important ideas for mentors and mentees to discuss. While an idea might start as a hunch or intuition, you should seek to support your ideas with evidence. If your ideas change or are influenced by the ideas and data of others, state how you modified your original idea and why.

5. **Pay attention to yourself and others:** Ideas don't exchange themselves. They are shared by people, each with his or her own goals, moods, and styles of learning and self-expression. Pay careful attention to how your own ideas and emotions, as well of those around you, are affecting the dialogue.

6. **Presume positive intentions:** Honest conversation requires that participants believe in each other's positive intentions. When you presume that colleagues share your goals for learning and professional growth, you are less likely to interpret their comments as threats or challenges.

7. **Pursue a balance between advocacy and inquiry:** Strive to spend as much time and energy inquiring into the ideas of others as you do in advocating for your own ideas.

ACTIVITY 1-1

NORMS OF COLLABORATION INVENTORY

Directions: Before your first meeting, rate yourself on each of the norms and their descriptions. Use your data to set goals, either individually or with your partner, to practice the skills in the context of your mentoring relationship. After future meetings, assess your progress in adopting the norms and share your responses with your partners, and with a study group if appropriate, to see how you or your group improved.

Name:_____ **Date:**_____

Purpose of Meeting:_____

Targeted Goal/s:_____

Norm	Rarely	Occasionally	Frequently
PAUSING			
♦ I allow time for thought after asking questions or making responses			
♦ I allow time before responding to others			
♦ I wait until others are finished before talking			
PARAPHRASING			
♦ I listen to the content & emotion of the speaker			
♦ I use a variety of reflective stems to summarize and organize the content of the speaker			
♦ I use non-verbal affirmations to signal agreement			
PROBING			
♦ I seek agreement on what words or concepts mean			
♦ I ask questions to clarify facts, ideas and stories			
♦ I ask questions to surface assumptions, points of view, beliefs, values, and rules of individuals and groups			
PUTTING IDEAS ON THE TABLE & PULLING THEM OFF			
♦ I state the intention of my communication			
♦ I reveal all relevant information with supporting facts when they are available			
♦ I explain reasons behind statements, questions and actions			
♦ I remove or announce the modification of my own ideas, opinions, points of view			
PAYING ATTENTION TO SELF & OTHERS			
♦ I maintain awareness of my thoughts and feelings			
♦ I maintain awareness of the group's task, mood and relevance of my own & other's contributions			
PRESUMING POSITIVE INTENTIONS			
♦ I act as if others mean well when responding to and inquiring of others			
♦ I restrain any emotional outbursts			
PURSUING BALANCE BETWEEN ADVOCACY & INQUIRY			
♦ I seek a balance between advocating my own ideas and inquiring into those of others			
♦ I present a rationale for positions, including assumptions, facts, and feelings			
♦ I disagree respectfully and openly with ideas and offer a rationale for my disagreement			
♦ I ask others their reasons for reaching and holding a position			

Adapted from Garmston, (1999)

ACTIVITY 1-2

REFLECTION INVENTORY

Directions: This activity asks you to think about your role as a teacher. Answer the following questions and share your responses with your partner. Use the Norms of Collaboration (Activity 1-1) to communicate your answers.

1. What am I most proud of in my work as a teacher?

2. What would I like my students to say about me when I'm out of the room?

3. What do I most need to learn about in my teaching?

4. What do I worry most about in my work as a teacher?

5. When do I know I've done good work?

6. What's the mistake I've made that I've learned the most from?

Pick one of these scenarios and take turns discussing what you would do.

1. Imagine a person who had never attended a traditional school decided to become a teacher and came to you asking to see good teaching in action. What would you tell that person to look for during a classroom visit?

2. You are serving on the "Teacher of the Year" award committee. What kinds of teacher actions would you use as the criteria for this award?

3. Think back to the last time you saw something happen that made you say, "This is great teaching." What did you see?

ACTIVITY 1-3

ROLE MODEL PROFILE

Directions: This activity asks you to think about teachers you had when you were a student, or colleagues with whom you have worked. Answer the following questions and share your responses with your partner. Use the Norms of Collaboration (Activity 1-1) to communicate your answers.

1. Think about the teachers you have known. Which ones best represent what a teacher should be? How did their teaching affect you?

2. What characteristics did you observe that make you feel that they were quality teachers?

3. How did other students respond to those teachers?

4. Which of those teachers' abilities would you most like to be able to borrow and integrate into your own teaching?

ACTIVITY 1-4

PARTNER INTERVIEW

Directions: Using the Norms of Collaboration (Activity 1-1), answer and discuss the following prompts with your partner.

1. Provide three pieces of professional information about yourself. . .

2. . . . and two pieces of personal information.

3. Share one thing that you especially enjoy doing, or at which you are particularly successful.

4. How are these things connected to your teaching and to your success in helping students learn?

REQUIRED FORMS SECTION

Monthly Seminar Planning Form

Partners use this form to select which monthly activities each would like to focus on at the monthly seminar. The coordinator collects this form and plans the seminars based on the feedback of participants.

Weekly Teacher Reflection Journal (duplicate as needed)

Each partner completes this form at the end of the week by taking 10 – 15 minutes to answer the reflection prompts. The weekly sheets are saved and used to complete the *Monthly Reflection Journal Summary*.

Monthly Reflection Journal Summary

Each partner completes this form prior to the monthly seminar meeting. The summary is used for dialogue and discussion with partners or groups. This sheet is saved every month.

Monthly Support Seminar Evaluation

Participants complete this form after the monthly support seminars. The coordinator collects and keeps these for ongoing assessment and revision of the mentor program.

MONTHLY SEMINAR PLANNING FORM

Date _____

Mentor Name _____

Mentee Name _____

Monthly Seminar Topic _____

I have reviewed this month's suggested activities and would like to focus on the following partner or small group activity:

Activity Number _____

Title _____

Mentee or Mentor Name _____

**WEEKLY TEACHER REFLECTION JOURNAL
AND MONTHLY REFLECTION JOURNAL SUMMARY**

Notes on Keeping a Teaching Journal:

Keeping a journal of the important events in your life as a teacher is a way to help you realize many things about yourself. Through regular writing and reading in your journal, you'll start to see patterns of thoughts and ideas about teaching. You'll become more aware of your habits and have a clearer understanding of your daily teaching practice. You'll become aware of how you organize your teaching, recognize your teaching strengths, and determine those skills that require more learning and practice. You will identify how your students influence your teaching, and discover ways to adapt, modify, and respond to their behavior to increase their success in the classroom. You will see patterns of emotional highs and lows and begin to identify factors related to them. Eventually, you will use this valuable resource to create a professional growth plan to improve your professional practice. In summary, a teaching journal is a tool that can lead to life-long learning for you, and to greater learning for your pupils.

The *Weekly Teacher Reflection Journal* is required as a weekly activity and is used throughout the mentor and mentee relationship as a means to ground future discussions and focus attention on the critical elements of teaching and student learning. The ability to reflect consciously on one's style of learning and adapt it to fit changing circumstances is central to the professional growth and development of an excellent teacher (Brookfield, 1987). Therefore, reflection through the *Weekly Teacher Reflection Journal* is the foundation for the work in each of the months to follow. Month One and Two will use these same four questions; in Months Three through Seven, questions will focus more specifically on the each month's topic.

DIRECTIONS

Spend 15-20 minutes a week writing in your *Weekly Teacher Reflection Journal*. Jot down your responses to the questions. These questions will focus on events you experienced and also events based on student responses. You may choose to highlight certain words or note patterns of behavior that help you identify strengths and areas for improvement. These weekly reflections are to be summarized individually on the *Monthy Reflection Journal Summary* form prior to the monthly seminar.

When you meet with your partner, bring your *Monthly Reflection Journal Summary* to use as a tool to analyze, assess, and reflect on your teaching and its effect on your students. Arrange a time to talk about what you've written. Save the *Monthly Reflection Journal Summary* each month; you will use it to set professional development goals and write a plan in Months Eight and Nine. The *Weekly Teacher Reflection Journal* and the *Monthly Reflection Journal Summary* forms are at the end of each month's activities in the Required Forms Section. Feel free to duplicate them as needed.

WEEKLY TEACHER REFLECTION JOURNAL

(Duplicate as needed)

Name: Date:

1. When did I feel the most connected, engaged, or affirmed as a teacher this week? When did I feel most confident and competent with my skills?

2. When did I feel the most disconnected, disengaged, or discouraged as a teacher this week? When did I doubt my competence and confidence?

3. If I could repeat this week, what would I do differently based on the learning and responses of my students?

4. What am I most proud of this week based on the learning and responses of my students?

5. Other thoughts about this week:

MONTHLY REFLECTION JOURNAL SUMMARY

Introducing the Mentoring Partners to the Reflective Process

Directions: Look at your current and previous responses to the prompts in your weekly reflection journal. Use a highlighter to find themes or patterns to your responses about each question. Summarize your entries under each of the prompts. Save this sheet!

1. Summarize the situations where you felt the most connected, engaged, or affirmed as a teacher this month. Summarize situations where you felt the most confident and competent.

Connected, Engaged, Affirmed	Confident and Competent with Skills

2. Summarize the situations where you felt the most disconnected, disengaged, or discouraged as a teacher this month. Summarize when you doubted your competence and confidence.

Disconnected, Disengaged, Discouraged	Not Confident and Competent with Skills

3. Summarize what you would do differently based on student learning and responses for the month.

Student Learning and Responses	What I'd Do Differently

4. Summarize what you are most proud of this month based on student learning and responses.

Student Learning and Responses	What I'm most proud of

MONTHLY SUPPORT SEMINAR EVALUATION
MONTH/TOPIC:

1. List the activity you chose to focus on this month:

2. List the learning partner(s) you worked with to complete this activity:

3. What was the most important thing you learned about this month's topic?

4. How has this month's activity influenced your classroom teaching?

5. What other monthly activities included in this chapter do you plan to complete?

6. What data will you collect as a result of this month's activity?

7. What suggestions do you have for improving the monthly seminars?

Month Two

EXPLORING OUR CURRENT REALITY

*Genuine beginnings begin within us, even when they are
brought to our attention by external opportunities.*
William Bridges

INTRODUCTION TO MONTH TWO

Now that mentors and mentees have had a chance to get acquainted as learning partners, they begin this month to explore two aspects of their current reality: their teaching environment, that is, the district, school and student body; and their own needs for professional development. Why is this helpful? The first step in finding the path to our goal is to know where we're starting from and how far we have to go. The realities of the challenges that face us, as well as our own abilities and needs, will define the knowledge, skills, and attitudes we need to acquire in order to become successful.

The context for teaching is larger than the individual classroom. Teachers are, first and foremost, employees of the school district and are expected to abide by district policies and procedures. Therefore, it is important to know the district's philosophy, goals, policies, rules, regulations, curriculum, and assessment requirements. In addition, schools are responsible to the citizens of the local community. Information about the community can be influential in the decisions of every teacher. The District/School/Classroom Inventory (Activity 2-1) is used to collect information about the district and the community it serves. Part of the exercise involves creating a list of people at the district or school that teachers can contact for assistance. This information will help the mentor and mentee in collaborative planning and decision making. It helps the partners answer crucial questions:

- What are the policies, procedures and regulations I must follow as a district employee?

- What are the philosophy and mission of the district and school?

- What are the district's academic standards and curriculum for students?

- What resources are available to me, and how do I access them?

- How can I use this information to become successful with all my students?

Along with understanding the external context of the school environment, the mentor and mentee must also identify their own needs early in their relationship so that both may plan for a successful learning partnership. A comprehensive needs assessment is included in Activity 2-2 and 2-3 for each to fill out, either individually or as partners. Activity 2-4 provides a template for planning to address those needs as learning partners in the coming months. The plan also identifies supports, resources, and personnel the partners will need to draw on. For example, a teacher may identify "understanding the curriculum" as a critical need. There may be several colleagues who can assist in meeting this goal, such as the principal, director of instruction, department heads, or teachers who were members of the curriculum committee. The teacher may wish to meet with one or plan lessons with another. This action plan clarifies the roles and expectations for each partner and helps them solve problems proactively.

LEARNING TARGETS

- Collect important district and school information to guide current and future decisions.

- Determine and plan for the needs of the mentor and mentee.

- Write each week in the *Weekly Teacher Reflection Journal*.

- Summarize weekly journal entries at the end of the month using *Monthly Reflection Journal Summary*.

RESOURCES

Distad, L. S., Chase, B., Germundsen, R., & Brownstein, J. C. (2000). Putting their heads together. *Journal of Staff Development, 21.* 49 – 51.

Garmston, R. J., & Wellman, B. M. (1999). *The adaptive school.* Norwood, MA: Christopher-Gordon Publishers, Inc.

Richardson, J. (April/May 2002). Take a closer look: Reflection gives educators the chance to tap into what they've learned. *Tools for Schools.* Oxford, OH: National Staff Development Council.

Senge, P. (2000). *Schools that learn.* New York: Doubleday.

Wong, H. K., & Wong, R. T. (1991) *The first days of school.* Sunnyvale, CA: Harry Wong Publishers.

Zeichner, K., Klehr, M., & Caro-Bruce, C. (2000). Pulling their own levers. *Journal of Staff Development, 21.* 36-39.

MONTH TWO SUPPORT SEMINAR ACTIVITIES

Number	Activity	Completed Date
	REQUIRED ACTIVITIES • Monthly Seminar Planning Form • Weekly Teacher Reflection Journal • Monthly Reflection Journal Summary • Monthly Support Seminar Evaluation	
2-1	**District/School/Classroom Inventory** **Purpose:** To collect information required for planning and preparation **Materials:** Activity worksheet 2-1 (may use district handbook & other resources that would assist) **Who:** Mentee assisted by Mentor as well as district employees, central office staff, and others who can provide the needed information. **Time:** Approximately 3 hours total to complete the inventory. Can be done in segments. 30 – 45 min. to share with the mentor and discuss how to use the information.	
2-2	**Needs Assessment (Mentee)** **Purpose:** Mentees assess their own needs for future planning with mentor. **Materials:** Activity worksheet 2-2 and Activity worksheet 2-4, pen/pencil **Who:** Mentee completes the initial assessment, and then meets with mentor to develop a plan (Activity worksheet 2-4). **Time:** Individual assessment = 10 – 15 min.	
2-3	**Needs Assessment (Mentor)** **Purpose:** To assess needs and write a plan of action that guides future activities. **Materials:** Activity worksheet 2-3 and Activity worksheet 2-4, pen/pencil **Who:** Mentor completes the initial assessment, then meets with mentee to develop a plan (Activity worksheet 2-4). **Time:** Individual assessment = 10 – 15 min.	
2-4	**Post-Assessment Action Plan** **Purpose:** To create a plan that meets the needs of both mentor and mentee after completing the needs assessment. **Materials:** Completed needs assessment worksheet 2-2 and 2-3 and Activity worksheet 2-4 **Who:** Mentor, mentee and other district personnel as needed **Time:** 1 hour	

ACTIVITY 2-1

DISTRICT/SCHOOL/CLASSROOM INVENTORY

SCHOOL DEMOGRAPHICS

1. How many students attend this school?

    Male: Female:

    Describe the student population in your school (range of cultural and socioeconomic diversity, ranges of ability, extracurricular activities, etc.). In general, how does this influence the climate of the school?

2. How would you describe the community or neighborhood? How might this influence your teaching (for example, the availability of classroom volunteers, parent speakers, field trips, peer tutors, etc.)?

3. List any other pertinent or interesting information regarding the location and population of the school.

DISTRICT/SCHOOL INFORMATION

4. What district and school policies and procedures must you observe as a professional?

DISTRICT	SCHOOL
Daily Policies (e.g., parking permits):	Daily Policies (e.g., attendance to office by 8:30):
Monthly Policies:	Monthly Policies:
Other:	Other:

5. What is the mission of the school and how does the school community support this mission? Does the faculty speak respectfully of the school's mission and strategic plans? What evidence do you observe that shows that the faculty and community support the mission or philosophy of the school?

6. Who can you go to for an explanation of the district, school and department, or grade level curriculum? What are the expectations regarding this curriculum?

7. Who can you go to for an explanation of the assessments and procedures required by the district and school?

8. List the names, email or phone of teachers at your grade level/department.

   Name _____ Email _____ Phone _____

   Name _____ Email _____ Phone _____

   Name _____ Email _____ Phone _____

   Name _____ Email _____ Phone _____

9. What other information from the district or school office do you need to be well informed about your professional responsibilities?

CLASSROOM/ STUDENT INFORMATION

10. How many students are in your class?

    Females: Males:

11. What student information do you need that will help you do effective lesson development, instruction, and curriculum planning for the year?

12. Which students require support from other personnel in your building or district?

13. What methods have you chosen to introduce yourself to:

    Parents:

    Students:

    Colleagues:

     Other:

14. What other information do you need to know about your students or their parents to guide your teaching?

DISTRICT/SCHOOL HUMAN RESOURCES

15. What programs are provided to students in this school/district? Check those provided and list the contact person, phone extension or email for contact.

_____Title I   Contact:_____

_____SAGE   Contact:_____

_____Special Education: Name and program title:
                    Contact:_____
                    Contact:_____
                    Contact:_____
                    Contact:_____
                    Contact:_____

_____ Non-English Language Learners: What language/s?
                    Contact:_____
                    Contact:_____

_____Peer Mentors   Contact:_____

_____Volunteers/Tutors
                    Contact:_____

_____Developmental Guidance
                    Contact:_____

_____School Psychologist
                    Contact:_____

_____Parent Liaison   Contact:_____

_____Liaison Officer Contact:_____

_____Paraprofessionals Contact:_____

_____School Nurse   Contact:_____

_____Other   Contact:_____

_____Other   Contact:_____

ACTIVITY 2-2

NEEDS ASSESSMENT FOR MENTEES
Part A.

For each item, write the letter in the rating column that most closely indicates your need for learning more in each area. Discuss your results with your mentor using the Norms of Collaboration (Activity 1-1). Create a collaborative plan for how to meet your needs (Activity 2-4).

A	B	C	D
Little Need for Learning	*Some* Need for Learning	*High Need* for Learning	*Very High* Need for Learning

Rating	Descriptor
	1. Using student data to drive instruction, planning, & assessment
	2. Understanding the academic standards and curriculum
	3. Planning & preparing for instruction
	4. Obtaining instructional resources and materials
	5. Using a variety of instructional methods
	6. Facilitating differentiated group instruction
	7. Assisting students with disabilities, ELL, etc.
	8. Organizing and managing my classroom
	9. Maintaining student rules and standards of behavior
	10. Motivating students
	11. Dealing with individual student differences
	12. Administering standardized achievement tests
	13. Using a variety of assessments to measure student learning
	14. Managing my time and work
	15. Dealing with stress
	16. Developing a professional growth plan based on professional teaching standards
	17. Finding out what is expected of me as a teacher/mentee
	18. Using the norms of collaboration for communication
	19. Communicating with administration and other colleagues
	20. Understanding the professional evaluation process
	21. Completing administrative paperwork
	22. Understanding my legal rights and responsibilities as a teacher
	23. Dealing with union-related issues
	24. Communicating with parents and community
	25. Knowing the special services provided by the district and community
	26. Other

Part B. Please respond to the following items

27. List any professional needs you have that are not addressed by the preceding items.

28. What support from the school district do you and other beginning teachers need?

ACTIVITY 2-3

NEEDS ASSESMENT FOR MENTORS

For each item, write the letter in the rating column that most closely indicates your need for learning more in each area. Discuss your results with your mentee using the Norms of Collaboration (Activity 1-1). Create a collaborative plan for how to meet your needs (Activity 2-4).

A	B	C	D
Little Need for Learning	*Some* Need for Learning	*High Need* for Learning	*Very High* Need for Learning

Rating	Descriptor
	1. Using student data to drive instruction, planning, & assessment
	2. Understanding the academic standards and curriculum
	3. Planning & preparing for instruction
	4. Obtaining instructional resources and materials
	5. Using a variety of instructional methods
	6. Facilitating differentiated group instruction
	7. Assisting students with disabilities, ELL, etc.
	8. Organizing and managing my classroom
	9. Maintaining student rules and standards of behavior
	10. Motivating students
	11. Dealing with individual student differences
	12. Administering standardized achievement tests
	13. Using a variety of assessments to measure student learning
	14. Managing my time and work
	15. Dealing with stress
	16. Developing a professional growth plan based on professional teaching standards
	17. Finding out what is expected of me as a teacher/mentee
	18. Using the norms of collaboration for communication
	19. Communicating with administration and other colleagues
	20. Understanding the professional evaluation process
	21. Completing administrative paperwork
	22. Understanding my legal rights and responsibilities as a teacher
	23. Dealing with union-related issues
	24. Communicating with parents and community
	25. Knowing the special services provided by the district and community
	26. Other

Part B. Please respond to the following items

27. List any professional needs you have that are not addressed by the preceding items.

28. What support from the school district do you and other beginning teachers need?

ACTIVITY 2-4

POST-ASSESSMENT ACTION PLAN

Directions: Use the information from your needs assessment to fill out your plan. An example is provided.

Name: _____ School: _____

Needs (Top 5 from Assessment 2-2 or 2-3)	Strategies/Actions to Meet Needs	Person/s or Resources to Assist (List names & how to locate)	Timeline To Meet Needs (Estimate dates)	Results
Understanding my legal rights and responsibilities as a teacher.	◆ Meet with my special education teacher to ask what's required of me in an IEP meeting ◆ Find out my legal obligations ◆ Find out who can support and help me with the parents	◆ Principal ◆ Director of Special Ed ◆ Special Ed Teacher	By my first IEP meeting next month	◆ Know my role in the IEP meeting and my responsibilities for accommodations for my students w/ disabilities
1.				
2.				
3.				
4.				
5.				

REQUIRED FORMS SECTION

Monthly Seminar Planning Form
Partners use this form to select which monthly activities each would like to focus on at the monthly seminar. The coordinator collects this form and plans the seminars based on the feedback of participants.

Weekly Teacher Reflection Journal (duplicate as needed)
Each partner completes this form at the end of the week by taking 10 – 15 minutes to answer the reflection prompts. The weekly sheets are saved and used to complete the *Monthly Reflection Journal Summary*.

Monthly Reflection Journal Summary
Each partner completes this form prior to the monthly seminar meeting. The summary is used for dialogue and discussion with partners or groups. This sheet is saved every month.

Monthly Support Seminar Evaluation
Participants complete this form after the monthly support seminars. The coordinator collects and keeps these for ongoing assessment and revision of the mentor program.

MONTHLY SEMINAR PLANNING FORM

Date _____

Mentor Name _____

Mentee Name _____

Monthly Seminar Topic _____

I have reviewed this month's suggested activities and would like to focus on the following partner or small group activity:

Activity Number _____

Title _____

Mentee or Mentor Name _____

WEEKLY REFLECTION TEACHER JOURNAL

(Duplicate as needed)

Name: Date:

1. When did I feel the most connected, engaged, or affirmed as a teacher this week? When did I feel most confident and competent with my skills?

2. When did I feel the most disconnected, disengaged, or discouraged as a teacher this week? When did I doubt my competence and confidence?

3. If I could repeat this week, what would I do differently based on the learning and responses of my students?

4. What am I most proud of this week based on the learning and responses of my students?

5. Other thoughts about this week:

Adapted from Brookfield, (1987)

MONTHLY REFLECTION JOURNAL SUMMARY

Introducing the Mentoring Partners to the Reflective Process

Directions: Look at your current and previous responses to the prompts in your weekly reflection journal. Use a highlighter to find themes or patterns to your responses about each question. Summarize your entries under each of the prompts. Save this sheet!

1. Summarize the situations where you felt the most connected, engaged, or affirmed as a teacher this month. Summarize situations where you felt the most confident and competent.

Connected, Engaged, Affirmed	Confident and Competent with Skills

2. Summarize the situations where you felt the most disconnected, disengaged, or discouraged as a teacher this month. Summarize when you doubted your competence and confidence.

Disconnected, Disengaged, Discouraged	Not Confident and Competent with Skills

3. Summarize what you would do differently based on student learning and responses for the month.

Student Learning and Responses	What I'd Do Differently

4. Summarize what you are most proud of this month based on student learning and responses.

Student Learning and Responses	What I'm most proud of

MONTHLY SUPPORT SEMINAR EVALUATION
MONTH/TOPIC:

1. List the activity you chose to focus on this month:

2. List the learning partner(s) you worked with to complete this activity:

3. What was the most important thing you learned about this month's topic?

4. How has this month's activity influenced your classroom teaching?

5. What other monthly activities included in this chapter do you plan to complete?

6. What data will you collect as a result of this month's activity?

7. What suggestions do you have for improving the monthly seminars?

Month Three

ANALYZING PROFESSIONAL PRACTICE

It is not because things are difficult that we do not dare;
it is because we do not dare that they are difficult.
Seneca

INTRODUCTION TO MONTH THREE

Professional teaching standards identify and describe the knowledge, skills, and attitudes that are the foundations of effective teaching practice. Teaching standards provide guidelines that allow all teaching professionals, novice or experienced, to share a common understanding of quality teaching. Constructed from the input and deliberation of many contributors, including teachers, the standards represent a broad consensus about what is important in teaching. Many states have developed and adopted their own teaching standards and use them for teacher licensure and evaluation. If your state has developed teaching standards, we encourage you to use them as the basis of your activities in Month Three.

This chapter introduces the National Board for Professional Teaching Standards (NBPTS), the standards that are used to assess teachers for National Board Certification. NBPTS is an education reform organization that sets high and rigorous standards for what teachers should know and be able to do in grades pre-K through 12. It was created so that teachers, like professionals in other fields, can achieve distinction by demonstrating mastery of specific standards through a demanding performance assessment. Classroom teachers and other educational professionals developed the NBPTS standards, with contributions from other disciplinary organizations. They represent a consensus of the teaching profession on what excellent teaching is in each of nearly thirty teaching specialties.

The NBPTS seeks to identify and recognize teachers who effectively enhance student learning and demonstrate a high level of knowledge, skills, abilities and commitments. These characteristics are embodied in the Five Core Propositions (NBPTS, 1999) that are at the heart of the National Board standards:

1. Teachers are committed to students and their learning. They act and believe that all students can learn.

2. Teachers know the subjects they teach and how to teach those subjects to students. Accomplished teachers have a rich understanding of the subject(s) they teach, as well as how the knowledge of their subject is created, organized, linked to other disciplines, and applied to real-world settings to create meaningful learning for students.

3. Teachers are responsible for managing and monitoring student learning. Accomplished teachers create, enrich, maintain, and alter instructional settings to capture and sustain the interest of their students while making the most effective use of time.

4. Teachers think systematically about their practice and learn from experience. Accomplished teachers critically examine their practice, seeking professional growth through advanced knowledge and principled judgment from their experiences.

5. Teachers are members of learning communities. Accomplished teachers continually make professional contributions towards the effectiveness of the school by working collaboratively with colleagues, parents, and the greater community.

The mentoring activities for Month Three are designed to reflect the Five Core Propositions by using the NBPTS Ten Fundamental Standards as a common reference.

Through dialogue and reflection on the standards, the mentor and mentee will create a "big picture" survey of their own professional practice in Activity 3-1. A sample survey is provided as a guide to help the partners search for and discuss excellent examples of each standard in their working environment. The learning partners collect artifacts (samples or products) of each standard in Activity 3-2 that can be used as exemplars for each of the standards. By examining and discussing these exemplars, the partners advance their understanding of the knowledge, skills and dispositions required for effective teaching.

In the *Weekly Teacher Reflection Journal* this month the learning partners will record their reflections on how the standards are applied in their every day teaching and how standards affect student learning.

LEARNING TARGETS

- Articulate the National Board Professional Teaching Standards or required state teaching standards and give examples of how the knowledge, skills, and dispositions expressed in the standards are related to professional growth and student learning.

- Focus the month's reflection in the *Weekly Teacher Reflection Journal* on observations and experiences related to the National Board standards and how they are applied in the everyday work of teaching and learning.

- Collect evidence that demonstrates the application of each standard. Partners will collect resources, examples, interviews, and other data in order to become more acquainted with the expectations of quality teaching embedded within each standard.

RESOURCES

Danielson, C. (1996). *Enhancing professional practice.* Alexandria, VA: ASCD.

Canter, L. & Canter, M. (1994). *Avoiding burnout and increasing your motivation.* Santa Monica, CA: Lee Canter & Assoc.

Guskey, T. R. *Evaluating professional development.* Thousand Oaks, CA: Corwin Press, Inc.

Goodlad, J. (1999). Renewing the profession of teaching. *Educational Leadership, 56.* 15-19.

Harman, A. E. (2001). A wider role for the national board. *Educational Leadership, 58.* 54-55.

Hole, S., & McEntee, G. H. (1999). Reflection is at the heart of practice. *Educational Leadership, 56.* 34-37.

Interstate New Teacher Assessment and Support Consortium (INTASC). (No date). *Draft standards for licensing beginning teachers.* Washington, D.C.: Council of Chief State Officers.

Journal of Staff Development, 20. (1999). Teacher quality.

Joyce, B., & Showers, B. (1995). *Student achievement through staff development.* White Plains, N. Y.: Longman Publications.

National Board for Professional Teaching Standards (1999). Southfield, MI: NBPTS. 1-800-22-TEACH.

Olebe, M., Jackson, A., & Danielson, C. (1999). Investing in beginning teachers – the California model. *Educational Leadership, 56.* 41-44.

Rogers, D. L., & Babinski, L. (1999). Breaking through isolation with new teacher groups. *Educational Leadership, 56.* 38-40.

Senge, P. (2000). *Schools that learn.* New York: Doubleday.

Wasley, P. (1999). Teaching worth celebrating. *Educational Leadership, 56.* 8-13.

Zachery, L. J. (2000). *The mentor's guide: Facilitating effective learning relationships.* San Francisco, CA.: Jossey-Bass.

MONTH THREE SUPPORT SEMINAR ACTIVITIES

Number	Activity	Completed Date
	REQUIRED ACTIVITIES • Monthly Seminar Planning Form • Weekly Teacher Reflection Journal • Monthly Reflection Journal Summary • Monthly Support Seminar Evaluation	
3-1	**Survey of NBPTS in the Workplace** **Purpose:** To develop a deeper understanding of how teaching standards are applied in the workplace. **Materials:** Activity worksheet 3-1 (or other descriptions of standards either required or preferred). **Who:** Mentor, Mentee (solicit support from building administrator or district curriculum director to conduct the investigation. Ask for good examples from the building, district or even other schools.). **Time:** 15 min. gather administrative support; 1 hr/week for 4 weeks maximum to collect information; 1 hour to discuss examples between mentor and mentee	
3-2	**Collecting Artifacts** **Purpose:** To collect evidence that demonstrates each of the standards in action. **Materials:** Activity worksheet 3-2 **Who:** Mentor and Mentee as partners. Can engage faculty, district professionals and others in seminars to collect and share artifacts. **Time:** One hour per week for four weeks. Less time if assigned to and divided among seminar participants or faculty to share.	

ACTIVITY 3-1

SURVEY OF NBPTS IN THE WORKPLACE

The goals of this activity are:

- to stimulate discussions between the learning partners and others about the qualities of excellent teaching
- to describe and define the importance of each teaching standard
- to explore and discuss excellent examples of each standard from observing and talking to practitioners in the building or district.

The survey guides the partners to explore the professional community and learn from the great examples of teachers within that community. When completed, this survey provides a valuable reference for more in-depth examination of the standards in later chapters.

The table uses NBPTS fundamental standards for partners to collect the information. However, if your state has adopted its own teaching standards, use those standards as the basis for these exercises. Other variations are listed below.

Variations:

- Go to www.nbpts.org for guides to certification in specialty areas. Use the descriptions to learn what specialty standards look like in action. Replace the NBPTS fundamental standards with specialty standards and look for examples of those standards in the workplace.

- Use the descriptions of domains and components from *A Framework for Teaching* by Charlotte Danielson as a guide to describe how the National Board standards are reflected in practice. Complete the survey, looking for authentic examples in the workplace.

- Seek someone who has achieved National Board Certification and discuss how the standards are applied to achieve this certification. Use some of the information to fill out the survey.

- Go to www.ccsso.org/intasc.html and replace the NBPTS fundamental standards with the ten standards from the Interstate New Teacher Assessment and Support Consortium (INTASC). Complete the survey, looking for authentic examples in the workplace.

ACTIVITY 3-1

SAMPLE SURVEY OF NBPTS IN THE WORKPLACE

Directions: Discuss the importance of each fundamental NBPTS standard with a learning partner or group of colleagues. Seek examples of each standard from the teachers in your school or district. Use this example as a guide.

NBPTS (Fundamental)	Why is this standard important for me? How does this affect student learning?	What resources (human, material, technological) can deepen my understanding of this?	Where can I see excellent examples of this in action?
I. Preparing for Productive Student Learning			
• Knowledge of Students	I have a very diverse group of students, many who receive special services this year. I will need some assistance to use this information in planning wisely.	Student surveys, office files, personal communication with colleagues and observations during class and professional literature	• Mr. Dooley's social studies class • Professional video library • Ask the principal • Special education teacher
• Subject-Matter Knowledge	My area is social studies but I am teaching one class in English composition. I need to know more for preparation of lessons.	• District curriculum & department head • Other teachers in the school	• English department student samples of work & lessons
• Knowledge & Use of Instructional Resources	I'd like to use more instructional technology to advance student work.	• Library media specialist • District inservices	• Mrs. Apple's English class
II. Advancing Student Learning in the Classroom			
• Learning Environment	Because my students have special needs, I want to structure the environment to be safe to take risks. Many students have not been successful in English.	Get samples of discipline plans but also ways to set clear expectations that students can achieve	• Ask the principal and other teachers. • Special education teacher
• Multiple Paths to Advance Learning	All students need to make progress based on where they are at the present moment. "One size doesn't fit all."	The learning specialist in the high school has strategies to use and has books I can borrow.	• Learning specialist can recommend examples of this
• Equity, Fairness, and Diversity	I have two students with limited English skills. I'll need assistance.	• Library media specialist • Spanish teacher	• Spanish emersion class
• Assessment	I will need help with district testing policy and procedures.	• Director of Instruction • Principal & other teachers	• My grade level team will help

III. Supporting Teaching & Student Learning

NBPTS (Fundamental)	Why is this standard important for me? How does this affect student learning?	What resources (human, material, technological) can deepen my understanding of this?	Where can I see excellent examples of this in action?
• Reflective Practice	I love the journal! It helps me focus on myself and students to improve.	• My mentor	• Discussions with my mentor
• Interaction w/ Professional Community	Team meetings are helpful for curriculum, instruction and student support.	• Team teachers	• Team meetings
• Interaction w/Families & the School's Community	My first conferences will be tough just because it's a first for me. I want students involved with parents.	• Mentor • Teachers who have student-parent conferences	• Video tape of how to run a conference with students

ACTIVITY 3-1

SURVEY OF NBPTS IN THE WORKPLACE

Directions: Discuss the importance of each fundamental NBPTS standard with a learning partner or group of colleagues. Seek examples of each standard from the teachers in your school or district. Save this as a reference for future activities. As appropriate, replace the NBTS Fundamental standards with standards for your state, or other applicable standards (see instructions).

NBPTS (Fundamental)	Why is this standard important for me? How does this affect student learning?	What resources (human, material, technological) can deepen my understanding of this?	Where can I see excellent examples of this in action?
I. Preparing for Productive Student Learning			
• Knowledge of Students			
• Subject-Matter Knowledge			
• Knowledge & Use of Instructional Resources			
II. Advancing Student Learning in the Classroom			
• Learning Environment			
• Multiple Paths to Advance Learning			
• Equity, Fairness, and Diversity			
• Assessment			

III. Supporting Teaching & Student Learning

NBPTS (Fundamental)	Why is this standard important for me? How does this affect student learning?	What resources (human, material, technological) can deepen my understanding of this?	Where can I see excellent examples of this in action?
• Reflective Practice			
• Interaction w/ Professional Community			
• Interaction w/Families & the School's Community			

ACTIVITY 3-2

SAMPLE FORM COLLECTING ARTIFACTS

Go on an archeological dig of artifacts (products or samples) that demonstrate mastery of each of the National Board standards. Use the example below as a guide for your discoveries. As appropriate, replace the NBTS Fundamental standards with standards for your state, or other applicable standards.

NBPTS (Fundamental)	ARTIFACT (Sample Product)	WHY I SELECTED THIS ITEM	HOW I'LL USE/ADAPT THIS ITEM
I. Preparing for Productive Student Learning			
• Knowledge of Students	Collect student surveys used by teachers for conferences.	Student information on interests can guide designs of lessons.	Let students know I will use their interests to guide their learning. I am genuinely interested.
• Subject-Matter Knowledge	Lessons plans from my department team	I admire one teacher for his enthusiasm about content and how he gets students engaged and learning.	I will look at how he plans and the resources he uses to develop engaging material for students.
• Knowledge & Use of Instructional Resources	List of differentiated instructional strategies used by Mrs. Honer	I'd like to try different strategies to reach all kids.	Apply different strategies to my instruction and observe student results.
II. Advancing Student Learning in the Classroom			
• Learning Environment	An sample of a good explanation of rules and consequences for students	I didn't have any college class in this area and am borrowing from other teachers to learn how to set structures for learning.	By using student feedback as data, I will revise and continue to get better at this area.
• Multiple Paths to Advance Learning	A list of different resources for our geography unit from the department head or library media specialist.	The text is too difficult for 25% of my students.	Allow choices for students to learn the concepts by having other resources available.
• Equity, Fairness, and Diversity	Differentiated lesson plans & instructional strategies	I have many students with variable abilities and attitudes about school I need assistance with this.	Not sure but I am experimenting with as many strategies as I can.
• Assessment	Portfolio designs.	It fits with my goals for meeting a variety of assessments for student needs.	I will keep a record of assessments used and learn how to use performance assessments in class.

III. Supporting Teaching & Student Learning

NBPTS (Fundamental)	ARTIFACT (Sample Product)	WHY I SELECTED THIS ITEM	HOW I'LL USE/ADAPT THIS ITEM
• Reflective Practice	*Weekly Teacher Reflection Journal*	I am enjoying the process of writing in this once a week.	I can see patterns of my strengths and needs.
• Interaction w/ Professional Community	Curriculum guides for meeting standards and how I use them.	I would like to learn how district curriculum is aligned with standards.	I can know what to teach and the prerequisites for the next grade.
• Interaction w/Families & the School's Community	Samples of letters home (especially ones in Spanish)	I want my communication to be friendly and effective with families of my students.	I can revise and develop letters based on the samples I collected.

ACTIVITY 3-3

COLLECTING ARTIFACTS

Go on an archeological dig of artifacts (products or samples) that demonstrate mastery of each of the National Board standards. As appropriate, replace the NBTS Fundamental standards with standards for your state, or other applicable standards.

NBPTS (Fundamental)	ARTIFACT (Sample)	WHY I SELECTED THIS ITEM	HOW I'LL USE/ADAPT THIS ITEM
I. Preparing for Productive Student Learning			
• Knowledge of Students			
• Subject-Matter Knowledge			
• Knowledge & Use of Instructional Resources			
II. Advancing Student Learning in the Classroom			
• Learning Environment			
• Multiple Paths to Advance Learning			
• Equity, Fairness, and Diversity			
• Assessment			

III. Supporting Teaching & Student Learning

NBPTS (Fundamental)	ARTIFACT (Sample)	WHY I SELECTED THIS ITEM	HOW I'LL USE/ADAPT THIS ITEM
• Reflective Practice			
• Interaction w/ Professional Community			
• Interaction w/Families & the School's Community			

REQUIRED FORMS SECTION

Monthly Seminar Planning Form

Partners use this form to select which monthly activities each would like to focus on at the monthly seminar. The coordinator collects this form and plans the seminars based on the feedback of participants.

Weekly Teacher Reflection Journal (duplicate as needed)

Each partner completes this form at the end of the week by taking 10 – 15 minutes to answer the reflection prompts. The weekly sheets are saved and used to complete the *Monthly Reflection Journal Summary*.

Monthly Reflection Journal Summary

Each partner completes this form prior to the monthly seminar meeting. The summary is used for dialogue and discussion with partners or groups. This sheet is saved every month.

Monthly Support Seminar Evaluation

Participants complete this form after the monthly support seminars. The coordinator collects and keeps these for ongoing assessment and revision of the mentor program.

MONTHLY SEMINAR PLANNING FORM

Date _____

Mentor Name _____

Mentee Name _____

Monthly Seminar Topic _____

I have reviewed this month's suggested activities and would like to focus on the following partner or small group activity:

Activity Number _____

Title _____

Mentee or Mentor Name _____

WEEKLY TEACHER REFLECTION JOURNAL

(Duplicate as needed)

Name: Date:

1. When did I feel the most connected, engaged, or affirmed as a teacher this week? When did I feel most confident and competent with my skills? What standards reflect my strengths this week?

2. When did I feel the most disconnected, disengaged, or discouraged as a teacher this week? When did I doubt my competence and confidence? What standards reflect my lack of competence and confidence?

3. If I could repeat this week, what would I do differently based on the learning and responses of my students? What standards reflect this?

4. What am I most proud of this week based on the learning and responses of my students? What standard/s reflect this?

5. Other thoughts about this week:

Adapted from Brookfield, (1987)

MONTHLY REFLECTION JOURNAL SUMMARY

Analyzing Professional Practice

Directions: Look at your current and past responses to the prompts in your weekly reflection journal. Use a highlighter to find themes or patterns to your responses about each question. Summarize your entries under each of the prompts. Save this sheet!

1.   Summarize the situations where you felt the most connected, engaged, or affirmed as a teacher this month. Summarize situations where you felt the most confident and competent.

Connected, Engaged, Affirmed	Confident and Competent with Skills

2.   Summarize the situations where you felt the most disconnected, disengaged, or discouraged as a teacher this month. Summarize when you doubted your competence and confidence.

Disconnected, Disengaged, Discouraged	Not Confident and Competent with Skills

3.   Summarize what you would do differently based on student learning and responses for the month.

Student Learning and Responses	What I'd Do Differently

4.   Summarize what you are most proud of this month based on student learning and responses.

Student Learning and Responses	What I'm most proud of

MONTHLY SUPPORT SEMINAR EVALUATION
MONTH/TOPIC:

1. List the activity you chose to focus on this month:

2. List the learning partner(s) you worked with to complete this activity:

3. What was the most important thing you learned about this month's topic?

4. How has this month's activity influenced your classroom teaching?

5. What other monthly activities included in this chapter do you plan to complete?

6. What data will you collect as a result of this month's activity?

7. What suggestions do you have for improving the monthly seminars?

Month Four

ANALYZING CLASSROOM ENVIRONMENT

A learning classroom requires methods and infrastructure that make it possible for everyone to foster one another's success deliberately. That means concentrating on changing the way people think and interact and recognizing that students learn in multiple ways and that their abilities are not fixed at birth. In such a class, students recognize that part of their purpose is making sure that everyone succeeds.

Peter Senge

INTRODUCTION TO MONTH FOUR

What is the most important factor in student learning? A 1994 meta-analysis of fifty years of research compared many factors – cognitive processes, home environment and parent support, school culture, curriculum design, school demographics, and others – and concluded that classroom management has the greatest effect on student learning (Wang, Haertel, & Walberg, 1994). It seems only logical that when we examine our professional practice we must first look at how we manage the classroom environment to foster learning for all students.

Yet, despite the crucial impact of the classroom environment on student learning, teachers often have no courses in classroom management prior to entering their profession. Some teachers are "naturals" when it comes to managing a classroom of students. They are able to structure the environment to meet the learning needs of a diverse student population and to regulate and adapt their strategies as they monitor student learning and behavior. Most teachers, however, must depend on trial and error, perhaps with the help of a few in-service programs or professional development courses. Often these programs are designed as one time, "sit-and-get" workshops that fail to include elements that have a greater impact on professional performance: on-the-job coaching, classroom observations, reflection, and follow-up to increase the teacher's skills. Mentoring is one of the best ways to equip new teachers with on-the-job examples and coaching to master the skills of creating, managing, and maintaining a learning environment.

In Month Four, the learning partners closely examine the NBPTS classroom management standard, a standard that reflects a broad agreement among teaching professionals about critical factors in establishing a learning environment. In addition to the NBPTS, the Interstate New Teacher Assessment and Support Consortium (INTASC) standards describe the knowledge, skills, and dispositions teachers need to create a learning environment (see Activity 4-4). Danielson (1996) added more descriptions, aligned the INTASC descriptors, and categorized them into six factors that encourage positive interactions, active engagement in learning, and self-motivation for students:

1. **Creating and maintaining standards for student behavior.** Students know the expectations for the quality of interactions and behavior in the classroom. Standards are discussed, agreed-upon, understood, and modeled, especially at the beginning of the year. Standards are consistently enforced in a fair and equitable manner. All standards are communicated to the parents for agreement and cooperation. This consistent communication and enforcement of behavior standards helps students feel emotionally safe.

2. **Creating a physical environment that engages the learning of all students.** The classroom is physically safe for students and designed for learning. Factors such as the arrangement of furniture for group or individual work, access to learning resources, use and position of equipment (overhead projector, screens, video equipment, etc.), design and placement of learning stations, and overall physical safety, are all directed toward meeting instructional goals.

3. **Creating a fair and respectful climate.** The teacher and students respect one another. Students demonstrate respect for each other and support each other in learning. Social interactions are positive and encouraged. Respect for student diversity is valued through the teacher's attention to student interests and abilities, as well as the fairness with which the teacher addresses individual learning needs.

4. **Creating an environment that results in positive social development and group responsibility.** The teacher uses appropriate developmental activities to teach and reinforce social and group responsibility. Students make decisions through offered choices on learning tasks. Classroom experiences are designed specifically to create a positive atmosphere. Students interact in a positive manner and can articulate to their parents how everyone gets along and works together.

5. **Creating classroom procedures and routines that support student learning.** Procedures that result in smooth operation of the classroom and efficient use of time are taught and rehearsed so that students can perform them properly. Movement in the classroom and management of routines are smooth and seamless. Students know what to do, and how and when to do it.

6. **Using instructional time effectively.** Students spend their time engaged in the learning tasks planned by the teacher. A focus on student learning predominates and interruptions are minimal.

Using student data to analyze the quality of learning in the classroom is the foundation of continuous professional growth. Data about student behavior is the primary resource teachers need to structure learning environments that promote a positive climate, productive work, purposeful learning, and quality interactions. Analyzing student feedback in light of the six factors helps teachers reflect on the positive and negative effects of each factor on the learning environment.

In turn, this analysis and reflection lets teachers know which classroom strategies are effective and which need to be adopted or strengthened. Ultimately, student results will determine whether or not the environment is conducive to learning. In this way, the classroom environment continually improves and changes to meet the changing needs of students; it becomes what Peter Senge (2000) calls a "learning classroom," one in which results lead to positive change.

This month's activities use Danielson's six factors as a focus to help the partners explore their current classroom management practices and compare them to best practices in the field in order to gain a deeper understanding of strategies to create classrooms that learn.

In Activity 4-1, the partners gather information about the six factors from a variety of resources, including colleagues in the building or district, readings from the resources listed at the end of this chapter, or online research. We provide an example of a completed form as a guide for collecting and using this information. As much as possible, authentic examples of each factor should be sought in the district or school where the learning partners work. The mentor or building principal may be the best guides to teachers who can model quality classroom management. Administrative support may be needed to provide release time for classroom observations and to help create an atmosphere where teachers openly welcome others to learn through their example. A keen sense of observation, inquiry, and analysis of student data is encouraged throughout all the activities for teacher reflection.

Activity 4-2 borrows from Wong's (1991) characteristics for effective classroom management to provide a self-assessment tool that aligns with the factors. This activity can be shared between the learning partners at the monthly seminar and can lead to focused writings in the *Weekly Teacher Reflection Journal*. The results of the activity can be saved to target goals for the professional development plan in Month Eight and Nine.

Preparation is one of the key factors in organizing and maintaining an effective classroom (Wong, 1991). Activity 4-3 serves as both a self-assessment and a learning tool that helps teachers identify strategies for classroom management and determine which strategies they need to reinforce in the classroom. The results can be used to target goals in Month Eight.

The teacher's knowledge, skills, and dispositions for creating a learning environment are the focus of Activity 4-4. After the learning partners reflect on these factors, the INTASC descriptor sheet stimulates discussion as they compare their answers.

Student data is the most important indicator of the effectiveness of the classroom environment. Activity 4-5 and 4-6 borrow Cummings's (2000) approach for action planning and problem solving to increase a student's self-discipline for learning.

The six factors of successful classrooms will be the focus of this month's *Weekly Teacher Reflection Journal* entries. Once they have completed their journal entries, the mentor and mentee will highlight their classroom management strengths and needs for improvement in the *Monthly Reflection Journal Summary* and save it for future use in Month Eight.

LEARNING TARGETS

- Use the six factors of successful classrooms to explore current classroom environments, identifying strengths and areas of need.

- Investigate and explore different classroom environment techniques and how they affect student learning.

- Set goals for creating a quality classroom environment based on the six factors, based on an analysis of reflections from the *Weekly Teacher Reflection Journal* and the *Monthly Reflection Journal Summary.*

RESOURCES (Arranged according to the six factors)**:**

1.   Creating and maintaining standards for student behavior

Canter, L., & Canter, M. (1994). *The high performing teacher: Avoiding burnout and increasing your motivation.* Santa Monica, CA.: Lee Canter & Assoc.

Cawleti, G. (Ed.) (1999). *Handbook of research on improving student achievement.* Arlington, VA: Educational Research Service.

Costa, A. L., & Kallick, B. (2000). *Discovering & exploring habits of mind.* Alexandria, VA: Association for Supervision and Curriculum Development.

Curwin, R. L. (1990). *Developing responsibility and self-discipline.* Santa Cruz, CA: ETR Associates.

Curwin, R. L., & Mendler, A. N. (1988). *Discipline with dignity.* Alexandria, VA: Association for Supervision and Curriculum Development.

Educational Leadership, 56 (1998). *Realizing a positive school climate.* Alexandria, VA: Association for Supervision and Curriculum Development.

Gossen, D. C. (1993). *Restitution: restructuring school discipline.* Chapel Hill, N.C.: New View Publications.

Interstate New Teacher Assessment and Support Consortium (INTASC). (No date). *Draft standards for licensing beginning teachers.* Washington, D.C.: Council of Chief State Officers.

Mendler, A. N. (1992). *What do I do when?* Bloomington, IN.: National Education Service.

Wong, H. K., & Wong, R. T. (1991). *The first days of school.* Sunnyvale, CA.: Harry Wong Publications.

2.   Creating a physical environment that engages the learning of all students

Cohen, E. G. (1994). *Designing groupwork.* New York: Teacher College Press.

Hart, L. A. (1983). *Human brain & human learning.* New York: Logman Pub.

Loomans, D., & Kolberg, K. (1993). *The laughing classroom.* Tiburon, CA: H J Kramer Inc.

McCarthy, B. (1996). *About learning.* Barrington, IL: Excel, Inc.

Caine, R. N., & Caine, G. (1991). *Making connections: Teaching and the human brain*. New York: Addison-Wesley.

Sylwester, R. (1995). *A celebration of neurons*. Alexandria, VA: Association for Supervision and Curriculum Development.

3. Creating a fair and respectful climate

Armstrong, T. (1999). *ADD/ADHD alternatives in the classroom*. Alexandria, VA: Association for Supervision and Curriculum Development.

Armstrong, T. (1998). *Awakening genius in the classroom*. Alexandria, VA: Association for Supervision and Curriculum Development.

Brendtro, L. K., Brokenleg, M., & Van Bockern, S. (1990). *Reclaiming youth at risk*. Bloomington, IN: National Education Service.

Donnellan, A. M., LaVigna, G. W., Negri-Schultz, N., & Fassbender, L. L. (1988). *Progress without punishment: Effective approaches for learners with behavior problems*. New York: Teachers College Press.

Kashani, J. H., Ray, J. S., & Carlson, G. A. (1984). Depression and depressive-like states in preschool-age children in a child development unit. *School Psychology Review*, 19. 196-211.

Kohn, A. (1996). *Beyond discipline: From compliance to community*. Alexandria, VA: Association for Supervision and Curriculum Development.

Meichenbaum, D., & Biemiller, A. (1998). *Nurturing independent learners: Helping students take charge of their learning*. Cambridge, MA: Brookline Books.

Payne, R. (1998). *A framework for understanding poverty*. Baytown, TX: RFT Publishing.

Seagal, S., & Horne, D. (1997). *Human dynamics*. Waltham, MA: Pegasus Press.

Stark, K. D. (1990). *The treatment of depression during childhood: A school-based program*. New York: Guilford Press.

4. Creating an environment that results in positive social development and group responsibility

Bocchino, R. (1999). *Emotional literacy: To be a different kind of smart.* Thousand Oaks, CA: Corwin Press.

Canfield, J. & Wells, H. C. (1994). *One hundred ways to enhance self-concept in the classroom.* New York: Allyn & Bacon.

Canfield, J., & Siccone, F. (1993). *One hundred one ways to develop student self-esteem & responsibility, Vol. I.* New York: Allyn & Bacon.

Gibbs, J. (2000). *Tribes: A new way of learning and being together.* Sausalito, CA: CenterSource Systems, LLC.

Glasser, W. (1993). *The quality school teacher.* New York: Harper.

Johnson, D. W., & Johnson, R. T. (1995). *Reducing school violence through conflict resolution.* Alexandria, VA: Association for Supervision and Curriculum Development.

Kessler, R. (2000). *The soul of education: helping students find connection, compassion, & character at school.* Alexandria, VA: Association for Supervision and Curriculum Development.

Kohn, A. (1990). *The brighter side of human nature.* New York: Harper Collins Publishers.

Raffini, J. P. (1993). *Winners without losers.* New York: Allyn Bacon.

Siccone, F., & Canfield, J. (1993). *One hundred one ways to develop student self-esteem & responsibility, Vol. II.* New York: Allyn & Bacon.

5. Creating classroom procedures and routines that support student learning

Caine, G., Caine, R. N. & Crowell, S. (1994). *Mindshifts: A brain-based process for restructuring schools and renewing education.* Tucson, AZ: Zypher Press.

Jensen, E. (1995). *Brain-based learning & teaching.* Del Mar, CA.: Turning Point Publishing.

National Center for Educational Statistics (1999, January). *Teacher quality: A report on the preparation and quality of public school teachers*. U.S. Department of Education.

Raffini, J. P. (1996). *One hundred fifty ways to increase intrinsic motivation in the classroom*. New York: Allyn & Bacon.

Scheidecker, D., & Freeman, W. (1999). *Bringing out the best in students: How legendary teachers motivate kids*. Thousand Oaks, CA: Corwin Press.

Wang, M., Haertel, G., & Walberg, H. (1994). What helps students learn? *Educational Leadership*, 51. (4), 74-79.

6. Using instructional time effectively

Brooks, J. G. & Brooks, M. G. (1993). *In search of understanding: The case for constructivist classrooms*. Alexandria, VA: Association for Supervision and Curriculum Development.

Cummings, C. (2000). *Winning strategies for classroom management*. Alexandria, VA: Association for Supervision and Curriculum Development.

Rogers, S., Ludington, J., & Graham, S. (1997). *Motivation & learning*. Evergreen, CO: Peak Learning Systems.

Secretary's Commission on Achieving Necessary Skills (1991). *What work requires of schools: A SCANS report for America 2000*. U.S. Department of Labor.

Zemelman, S., Daniels, H., & Hyde, A. (1998). *Best practice: New standards for teaching & learning in America's schools*. Portsmouth, NH: Heinemann.

MONTH FOUR SUPPORT SEMINAR ACTIVITIES

Number	Activity	Completed Date
	REQUIRED ACTIVITIES • Monthly Seminar Planning Form • Weekly Teacher Reflection Journal • Monthly Reflection Journal Summary • Monthly Support Seminar Evaluation	
4-1	**Classroom Environment Data Gathering** **Purpose:** To observe authentic, on-the-job examples of the six factors. **Materials:** Activity worksheet 4-1 and a list of teachers for classroom observation. Time should be scheduled to meet and discuss classroom strategies with the teachers they have observed. **Who:** Ideally, mentor and mentee should work as learning partners. Can be done individually by each and shared later for comparison and discussion. **Time:** 1 hour/week to collect examples; 30 – 45 minutes to share and analyze results	
4-2	**Survey of the Classroom Environment** **Purpose:** To assess current level of proficiency in managing student learning behavior in the classroom. **Materials:** Activity worksheet 4-2, pen/pencil **Who:** Analyze individually **Time:** 45 min. – 1 hr. to do the self assessment; 30 – 45 min. to share with mentor/mentee	
4-3	**Strategies for Effective Discipline** **Purpose:** To assess and discuss strategies for effective classroom discipline. **Materials:** Activity worksheet 4-3, pen/pencil **Who:** Mentee, Mentor or identified group in seminar **Time:** 1 hour to reflect, assess and discuss	

Number	Activity	Completed Date
4-4	**Creating a Learning Environment:** **Teacher Knowledge, Skills and Dispositions** **Purpose:** To identify, compare, and discuss the teacher's self-identified characteristics with the INTASC teacher descriptions. **Materials:** Activity worksheet 4-4, pen/pencil **Who:** Mentor and mentee as learning partners, small group of teachers in seminar **Time:** 45 minutes total	
4-5	**Student Goal Setting Template** **Purpose:** To create annual learning and behavior goals for students. **Materials:** Activity worksheet 4-5, pen/pencil (can use markers and visual mapping with younger students) **Who:** Both mentor and mentee with class or individual students **Time:** 1 hour	
4-6	**Problem Solving Template** **Purpose:** To create student responsibility to solve classroom and behavioral problems. **Materials:** Activity worksheet 4-6 **Who:** Mentor or Mentee with individual students **Time:** 30 – 45 min.	

ACTIVITY 4-1

CLASSROOM ENVIRONMENT DATA GATHERING

Directions: Investigate and explore excellent examples of each of the factors by gathering information from different sources. Complete the chart and share with your learning partner. Use the sample chart on the next page as a guide for your observations.

Factors	Source of information (interview with teacher, observation of class, reading, online chat, etc.)	What I learned	How it can change my classroom management
1. Creating and maintaining standards for student behavior			
2. Creating a physical environment that engages the learning of all students			
3. Creating a fair and respectful climate			
4. Creating an environment that results in positive social development and group responsibility			
5. Creating classroom procedures and routines that support student learning			
6. Using instructional time effectively			

ACTIVITY 4-1

SAMPLE CLASSROOM ENVIRONMENT DATA SHEET

Factors	Source of information (interview with teacher, observation of class, reading, online chat, etc.)	What I learned	How it can change my classroom management
1. Creating and maintaining standards for student behavior	The First Days of School, Chapter 18. Mrs. Dumphy's class 3rd hour for observation.	How to develop a discipline plan and enforce rules consistently. Mrs. Dumphy's class uses Tribes for standards.	I need consistent enforcement of rules without thinking I'm not in control. I want to take a Tribes training.
2. Creating a physical environment that engages the learning of all students	Mr. Will uses learning stations. I will observe his use of these with all students.	Learning stations allows students choice without chaos. Each station has group sign-up and expectations that are monitored by both students and Mr. Will.	I don't feel comfortable with learning stations yet, but asked Mr. Will to work with me on a unit second semester so I can try it.
3. Creating a fair and respectful climate	I will speak with the guidance counselor who has Tribes training and has done some developmental guidance activities.	Fair does not mean equal. Students need to understand differences for some students.	I have rules everyone must obey, but need to accommodate students with disabilities, most especially those with behavior problems.
4. Creating an environment that results in positive social development and group responsibility	I want to see examples of teachers who do this with ease. I will ask the principal and my mentor for examples. I can use the resources listed in this section, too.	I found several activities that develop group responsibility and problem solving. I want to see a teacher use these in the classroom. I will try one but keep looking for examples.	I need to feel more confident in giving students more choices but don't know how to structure that without thinking they'll take advantage of me.
5. Creating classroom procedures and routines that support student learning	I will ask my mentor to observe me. I think I'm pretty good at this because there aren't a lot of disruptions or confusion with attendance, transitions, etc.	We didn't have time this month. Too much going on! Maybe next month!	
6. Using instructional time effectively	Argh! I need lots of help. I'm getting a list of resources, teachers, ANYTHING. This may be a life-long goal!	Ms. F. Ishint chunks her instruction with some time for large group, some for projects, some for group interaction and some independent.	I keep thinking I have to be "in charge" and do all the instruction. I need more help with group activities!

ACTIVITY 4-2

SURVEY OF THE CLASSROOM ENVIRONMENT

Directions: Circle the number that corresponds to your effectiveness on each of the characteristics below. Include the comments and insights about your performance that led to your assessment.

Characteristics	Effective Teacher			Ineffective Teacher	Comments & Insights
1. High level of student involvement with work & content	4 Students are working and engaged in the content.	3	2	1 Teacher is working hard to keep students on task.	
2. Clear student expectations	4 Students know that assignments are based on standards & high expectations for success.	3	2	1 Teacher assigns the chapter in a text and tells students to know the material.	
	4 Students know how & why they are assessed.	3	2	1 Teacher is vague and unclear about what students will need to know and do to succeed.	
3. Relatively little wasted time & confusion	4 Teacher has a discipline plan.	3	2	1 Teacher makes up rules and punishes according to his/her mood.	
	4 Teacher starts class immediately.	3	2	1 Teacher takes roll and dallies.	
	4 Teacher posts assignments.	3	2	1 Students ask or don't know the assignments.	

ACTIVITY 4-2

SURVEY OF THE CLASSROOM ENVIRONMENT

Directions: Circle the number that corresponds to your effectiveness on each of the characteristics below. Include the comments and insights about your performance that led to your assessment.

Characteristics	Effective Teacher		Ineffective Teacher		Comments & Insights
4. Work-oriented but relaxed and pleasant climate	4 Teacher has invested time in practicing procedures until they are routine.	3	2	1 Teacher tells but does not rehearse procedures.	
	4 Teacher brings the class to attention efficiently.	3	2	1 Teacher spends too much time trying to get students' attention with little success.	
	4 Teacher uses recognition & encouragement of student performances.	3	2	1 Teacher uses generalized praise or none at all.	

ACTIVITY 4-3

STRATEGIES FOR EFFECTIVE DISCIPLINE

Rate yourself from 4 to 1 (4 being very effective) on the strategies for effective discipline. Discuss your rating with your learning partner, focusing on those that are of most concern or interest to you.

Strategies for Effective Discipline	Effective			Need Help
1. My discipline plan minimizes classroom disturbances and maximizes learning.	4	3	2	1
2. I have a well-ordered environment with high academic expectations.	4	3	2	1
3. My rules prevent or encourage behavior by clearly stating expectations for students.	4	3	2	1
4. My rules are limited to a number that the students can readily remember – never more than five.	4	3	2	1
5. My rules are written, permanently posted in the classroom, and given to students on paper or copied into their notebook.	4	3	2	1
6. To establish student responsibility for standards of behavior, I discuss with the students why rules are needed and how rules help them succeed. I establish specific examples of general rules such as "respect others".	4	3	2	1
7. I notice that students will swiftly violate a rule that others are violating if the rule is not enforced.	4	3	2	1
8. Students often observe that I do mean what I say.	4	3	2	1
9. My consequences are reasonable and logical. A reasonable consequence follows logically from the behavior and is not arbitrarily imposed.	4	3	2	1
10. I do not stop instruction when I enforce a rule.	4	3	2	1
11. When I see a violation of the rules, I immediately give out the penalty.	4	3	2	1
12. I give out the penalty quietly as I continue with the lesson or class-work.	4	3	2	1
13. I present my discipline plan to my administrator and tell him/her what I plan to do when students break a rule.	4	3	2	1
14. I give parents a copy of my discipline plan and ask for their cooperation as I enforce it.	4	3	2	1
15. I give specific descriptions to the student of the behavior I am witnessing rather than labeling the student as "unmotivated", "disruptive" or "lazy".	4	3	2	1
16. I post my rewards and when they will be granted (for instance, immediately, daily or weekly).	4	3	2	1

Strategies for Effective Discipline	Effective			Need Help
17. I understand that most behavior problems in the classroom are caused by the failure of students to follow procedures and routines.	4	3	2	1
18. I can run my class smoothly because I teach procedures to the students.	4	3	2	1
19. My procedures are taught through explaining, rehearsing and reinforcing.	4	3	2	1
20. My procedures for each activity are taught early in the year.	4	3	2	1
21. My class is task-oriented and predictable.	4	3	2	1
22. I understand the importance of using proximity to students.	4	3	2	1
23. I use proximity to materials to increase efficiency of getting what students need to work on assignments.	4	3	2	1
24. I create and maintain a climate of fairness and respect.	4	3	2	1
25. I spend time up front thinking about classroom management.	4	3	2	1
26. I seat students purposefully for accomplishing the tasks I assign.	4	3	2	1
27. I design different seating arrangements based on the purpose of the assignments.	4	3	2	1
28. Overall, I feel I can create and maintain a healthy classroom learning environment.	4	3	2	1

Adapted from Wong & Wong, 1991, *The First Days of School.*

MONTH FOUR

ACTIVITY 4-4

CREATING A LEARNING ENVIRONMENT:
TEACHER KNOWLEDGE, SKILLS AND DISPOSITIONS

Directions: With a partner or small group, fill in the three columns with what you believe are the knowledge, skills, and dispositions teachers need to create and maintain a learning environment. When you are finished, compare your answers with the INTASC characteristics on the next page. Share your comparisons with your partner or group.

Knowledge (What do you need to know? What is the content to learn?)	Skills (What do you need to do? How do you apply the content in your classroom? How does it work?)	Dispositions (What are the attitudes, beliefs, or values about the learning environment that will make you and your students successful?)

INTASC Standard Five: Creating a Learning Environment

The teacher uses an understanding of individual and group motivation and behavior to create a learning environment that encourages positive social interaction, active engagement of learning, and self-motivation (INTASC, *Draft Standards for Licensing Beginning Teachers*).

Knowledge	Skills	Dispositions
• The teacher can use knowledge about human motivation and behavior drawn from the foundational sciences of psychology, anthropology, and sociology to develop strategies for organizing and supporting individual and group work.	• The teacher creates a smoothly functioning learning community in which students assume responsibility for themselves and one another, participate in decision making, work collaboratively and independently, and engage in purposeful learning activities.	• The teacher takes responsibility for establishing a positive climate in the classroom and participates in maintaining such a climate in the school as a whole.
• The teacher understands how social groups function and influence people, and how people influence groups.	• The teacher engages students in individual learning activities that help students develop the motivation to achieve, for example, relating lessons to students' personal interests, allowing students to have choices in their learning, and leading students to ask questions and pursue problems that are meaningful to them.	• The teacher understands how participation supports commitment and is committed to the expression and use of democratic values in the classroom.
• The teacher knows how to help people work productively and cooperatively with each other in complex social settings.		• The teacher values the role of students in promoting each other's learning and recognizes the importance of peer relationships in establishing a climate of learning.
• The teacher understands the principles of effective classroom management and can use a range of strategies to promote positive relationships, cooperation, and purposeful learning in the classroom.	• The teacher organizes, allocates, and manages the resources of time, space, activities, and attention to provide active and equitable engagement of students in productive tasks.	• The teacher recognizes the value of intrinsic motivation to students' lifelong growth and learning.
• The teacher recognizes factors and situations that are likely to promote or diminish intrinsic motivation, and knows how to help students become self-motivated.		• The teacher is committed to the continuous development of individual student's abilities and considers how different motivational strategies are likely to encourage this development for each student.

(See following page)

INTASC Standard Five: Creating a Learning Environment

The teacher uses an understanding of individual and group motivation and behavior to create a learning environment that encourages positive social interaction, active engagement of learning, and self-motivation (INTASC, *Draft Standards for Licensing Beginning Teachers*).

Knowledge	Skills	Dispositions
(See previous page)	(See previous page)	(See previous page)
	• The teacher maximizes the amount of class time spent in learning by creating expectations and processes for communication and behavior along with a physical setting conducive to classroom goals.	
	• The teacher helps the group develop shared values and expectations for student interactions, academic discussions, and individual and group responsibility that create a positive classroom climate of openness, mutual respect, support and inquiry.	
	• The teacher analyzes the classroom environment and makes decisions and adjustments to enhance social relationships, student motivation and engagement, and productive work.	
	• The teacher organizes, prepares students for, and monitors independent and group work that allows for full and varied participation of all individuals.	

ACTIVITY 4-5

STUDENT GOAL SETTING TEMPLATE

This template can be used to help students set goals for the year, or as a behavioral or academic intervention plan.

1. My goal: (state what it will look like when you are doing what you desire)

2. Action Steps to Reach My Goal:

    First I will do this:

    Then I will do this:

    Then I will do this:

    Then I will do this:

3. I will know I have accomplished my goal when:

4. Some things that may get in the way of my goal are:

    •
    •
    •

5. People or things that will help me achieve my goal:

6. Goal conference dates:

Adapted from Cummings, 2000, *Winning Strategies for Classroom Management*

ACTIVITY 4-6

PROBLEM SOLVING TEMPLATE

Directions: This template can be used with individuals or groups of students who need to resolve academic or behavioral issues. An example is provided below; you will find a blank template on the next page.

Problem: I am late for class at least 2 days a week because my locker is a mess and I can't find what I need for class.	
Solutions ("If")	**Consequences ("Then")**
1. If I kept my locker organized	then I could find what I needed in less time and be on time for class.
2. If I kept materials in my backpack instead of my locker	then I could be on time every day and just look for everything once I was in class.
3. If I got to school 15 minutes earlier	then I could find what I need in my locker and be on time for class.
4. If I didn't have to be to school on time	then I wouldn't be marked tardy! Ha Ha!

From Cummings, 2000, *Winning Strategies for Classroom Management*

ACTIVITY 4-6

PROBLEM SOLVING TEMPLATE

Directions: Use this template with individuals or groups of students to resolve academic or behavioral issues. Decide on the solutions that are doable and will create the most success.

Problem:	
Solutions ("If")	**Consequences ("Then")**
1.	1.
2.	2.
3.	3.
4.	4.

From Cummings, 2000, *Winning Strategies for Classroom Management*

REQUIRED FORMS SECTION

Monthly Seminar Planning Form

Partners use this form to select which monthly activities each would like to focus on at the monthly seminar. The coordinator collects this form and plans the seminars based on the feedback of participants.

Weekly Teacher Reflection Journal (duplicate as needed)

Each partner completes this form at the end of the week by taking 10 – 15 minutes to answer the reflection prompts. The weekly sheets are saved and used to complete the *Monthly Reflection Journal Summary*.

Monthly Reflection Journal Summary

Each partner completes this form prior to the monthly seminar meeting. The summary is used for dialogue and discussion with partners or groups. This sheet is saved every month.

Monthly Support Seminar Evaluation

Participants complete this form after the monthly support seminars. The coordinator collects and keeps these for ongoing assessment and revision of the mentor program.

MONTHLY SEMINAR PLANNING FORM

Date _____

Mentor Name _____

Mentee Name _____

Monthly Seminar Topic _____

I have reviewed this month's suggested activities and would like to focus on the following partner or small group activity:

Activity Number _____

Title _____

Mentee or Mentor Name _____

WEEKLY TEACHER REFLECTION JOURNAL

(Duplicate as needed)

Name: Date:

1. When did I feel the most connected, engaged, or affirmed as a teacher this week? When did I feel most confident and competent with my skills? What teaching standards are reflected in my skills?

2. When did I feel the most disconnected, disengaged, or discouraged as a teacher this week? When did I doubt my competence and confidence? What teaching standards are reflected in my lack of competence and confidence?

3. If I could repeat this week, what would I do differently based on the learning and response of my students? What teaching standards reflect this?

4. What am I most proud of this week based on the learning and responses of my students? Were there particular successes related to classroom management?

5. Other thoughts about this week:

MONTHLY REFLECTION JOURNAL SUMMARY

Analyzing Classroom Environment

Directions: Look at your current and past responses to the prompts in your weekly reflection journal. Use a highlighter to find themes or patterns in your responses to each question. Summarize your entries under each of the prompts. Save this sheet!

1.　Summarize the situations where you felt the most connected, engaged, or affirmed as a teacher this month. Summarize situations where you felt the most confident and competent.

Connected, Engaged, Affirmed	Confident and Competent with Skills

2.　Summarize the situations where you felt the most disconnected, disengaged, or discouraged as a teacher this month. Summarize when you doubted your competence and confidence.

Disconnected, Disengaged, Discouraged	Not Confident and Competent with Skills

3.　Summarize what you would do differently based on student learning and responses for the month.

Student Learning and Responses	What I'd Do Differently

4.　Summarize what you are most proud of this month based on student learning and responses.

Student Learning and Responses	What I'm most proud of

**MONTHLY SUPPORT SEMINAR EVALUATION
MONTH/TOPIC:**

1. List the activity you chose to focus on this month:

2. List the learning partner(s) you worked with to complete this activity:

3. What was the most important thing you learned about this month's topic?

4. How has this month's activity influenced your classroom teaching?

5. What other monthly activities included in this chapter do you plan to complete?

6. What data will you collect as a result of this month's activity?

7. What suggestions do you have for improving the monthly seminars?

Month Five

UNDERSTANDING ASSESSMENT

I have a dream that assessment...
...will be accepted as a means to help teachers plan instruction rather than as a contrivance to force teachers to jump through hoops;
...will be based on trust in teachers' judgment as much as numbers on a page are trusted;
...will become a helpful means to guide children to identify their own literacy strengths rather than a means to conveniently label them;
...will support each child in becoming the best he or she can be rather than a means to sort children into groups of the best and the worst;
And I have a dream that assessment will be put to use to honor what children can do rather than destroying them for what they can't do.
If we all work together we can make such dreams become a reality as we work to help each child grow.
Roger Farr

INTRODUCTION TO MONTH FIVE

A balanced assessment system can provide the necessary feedback that helps students learn and allows teachers to improve their practice. All too often, however, assessment is a narrow, unfocused process that seems punitive to both students and parents. To help students learn, assessment strategies must be appropriately matched to content and learning targets and aligned with content standards. The results must then be carefully analyzed and integrated into a plan for improved teaching and learning.

The activities presented this month help the mentee and mentor focus on key assessment issues. Each activity promotes reflective thought and dialogue around these essential questions:

1. What is it we expect students to learn and be able to do?
2. How will we know if and when students have learned?
3. How will we respond when students have not learned?

We urge all participants to complete Activity 5-1 as a way of exploring prior history and learning how past assessment experiences influence current teaching. Activities 5-2, 5-3, and 5-4 provide exercises that help establish a foundation for effective assessment practices.

Current research suggests that giving students regular writing assignments across content areas and using clearly written rubrics to score their writing improves overall student achievement and accelerates learning (Reeves, 2001; Wiggins, 1998). Activities 5-5 and 5-6 provide practice in developing writing prompts and using writing rubrics to score student writing samples.

Standardized testing is a common practice in most districts, and all teachers should be familiar with the valid purposes for standardized testing as well as its limitations. They particularly need to know about the standardized tests that are administered in their school, at which grade levels they are administered, and how the assessment results are used. Activity 5-7 provides a questionnaire to be completed by mentee and mentor to encourage meaningful dialogue and promote better understanding of the standardized assessments administered in the district.

As Guskey (1999) illustrates in his research, grading issues are especially challenging at the middle and high school levels. Activity 5-8 provides an exercise that promotes discussion about whether grades fairly and accurately assess student achievement.

Finally, Activity 5-9 is an assessment planning tool. The *Assessment Planning Matrix* will assist both mentee and mentor to plan a well-balanced assessment system that matches key skills, lessons and activities. Partners record their reflections on assessment and its role in student growth and learning in the *Weekly Teacher Reflection Journal*. Selected journal entries can be used as the focus of dialogue and discussion for mentor and mentee meetings as well as this month's support seminar.

LEARNING TARGETS

- Clearly define assessment expectations at the beginning of the lesson or unit of study and share them openly with students.
- Understand that assessment strategies are tools for providing learning feedback to both teacher and student.
- Use assessment strategies that help students see connections among lessons, units and courses.
- Connect the appropriate assessment methods with the skills we want students to learn and use.
- Plan assessments collaboratively with other learning partners.

RESOURCES:

Costa, L., & Kallick, B. (Eds.) (1995). *Assessment in the Learning Organization.* Alexandria, VA: Association for Supervision and Curriculum Development.

Educator in Connecticut's Pomperaug Regionat School District 15. (1996). *Performance-based learning and assessment.* Alexandria, VA: Association for Supervision and Curriculum Development.

Farr, R. (1997). *I have a dream about assessment: Developing a balanced assessment system.* Presentation at the Association of Supervision and Curriculum Development, Orlando, FL.

Guskey, T. (1999). *Using assessments to improve student learning.* Presentation at the National School Conference Institute, Las Vegas, NV.

Marzano, J. (2000). *Transforming Classroom Grading.* Alexandria, VA: Association for Supervision and Curriculum Development.

Reeves, D. (2001). *Standards are not enough: Essential transformations for successful schools.* Keynote address at the National School Conference Institute, Las Vegas, NV.

Rogers, S., & Graham, S. (1998). *The high performance toolbox.* Evergreen, CO: Peak Learning Systems.

Sargent, J.W., & Smejkal, A.E. (2000). *Targets for teachers: A self study guide for teachers in the age of standards.* Winnepeg, Canada: Portage & Main.

Stiggins, R., & Knight, T. (1997). *But are they learning?* Portland, OR: Assessment Training Institute.

Stiggins, J. (1997). *Student-centered classroom assessment.* Columbus, OH: Merrill Prentice Hall.

Strong, R., Silver, H., & Perini, M. (2001*). Teaching what matters most: Standards and strategies for raising student achievement.* Alexandria, VA: Association for Supervision and Curriculum Development.

Wiggins, G. (1998). *Educative assessment: Designing assessment to inform and improve student performance.* San Francisco: Jossey-Bass Publishers.

Wiggins, G., & McTighe, J. (1998). *Understanding by design.* Alexandria, VA: Association for Supervision and Curriculum Development.

MONTH FIVE SUPPORT SEMINAR ACTIVITIES

Number	Activity	Completed Date
	REQUIRED ACTIVITIES • Monthly Seminar Planning Form • Weekly Teacher Reflection Journal • Monthly Reflection Journal Summary • Monthly Support Seminar Evaluation	
5-1	**Examining Assessment History** **Purpose:** To understand how prior assessment experiences affect current attitudes and methods regarding assessment. **Materials:** Activity worksheet 5-1 **Who:** Mentor and mentee complete the questionnaire independently and then share the results with each other or in small groups during the support seminar meeting. **Time:** 60 minutes (30 minutes to complete and 30 minutes for sharing)	
5-2	**Assessment Literacy Inventory/Action Plan** **Purpose:** To determine strengths and areas for improvement related to assessment, and to develop an action plan to address assessment needs. **Materials:** Activity worksheet 5-2. The Assessment Literacy Inventory is offered in two parts. First, a rubric is introduced to help mentor and mentee each determine their own strengths and areas for improvement. Afterward, they meet and jointly develop an action plan based on the results of the rubric. **Who:** Mentor and mentee each complete independently, then share results with each other. **Time:** 90 minutes: 30 minutes to complete and 60 minutes for sharing results and completing the action plan.	

MONTH FIVE

Number	Activity	Completed Date
5-3	**Analyzing Best Assessment Methods** **Purpose:** To learn to identify the achievement target and standards within a specific lesson or unit and identify the best assessment method to demonstrate that students have met the achievement target. **Materials:** Activity worksheet 5-3 **Who:** Mentor and mentee working as partners **Time:** 2 hours	
5-4	**Analyzing Student Work** **Purpose:** To provide the opportunity to analyze the results of a whole-class assignment. **Materials:** One set of graded class assignments. **Who:** Mentor and mentee partners or small mixed groups of mentors and mentees **Time:** 1 – 2 hours	
5-5	**Constructed Response Activity** **Purpose:** To provide experience in using and evaluating the constructed response assessment method. **Materials:** Activity worksheets 5-5 **Who:** Mentor and mentee partners and/or small groups **Time:** 30 minutes	
5-6	**Using Writing Rubrics to Assess Student Writing Samples** **Purpose:** To give mentees and mentors experience with using writing rubrics to assess student writing samples. **Materials:** 4 to 6 classroom writing samples; Activity 5-6 writing rubrics (the appropriate grade level writing rubric will be needed for each writing sample; photocopy as needed). **Who:** Mentor and mentee partners and/or small groups **Time:** 30 – 60 minutes	

Number	Activity	Completed Date
5-7	**Examining District and/or State Standardized Assessment Systems** **Purpose:** To help mentees better understand the standardized assessment system in their district and how the results are used to improve student learning. **Materials:** Activity 5-7 questionnaire **Who:** Mentee and mentor partners or small mixed groups of mentees and mentors **Time:** 45 minutes	
5-8	**Examining Grading Issues** **Purpose:** To determine the extent to which grades fairly and accurately reflect student learning and achievement. **Materials:** Activity worksheet 5-8 **Who:** Mentor and mentee partners or small mixed groups of mentees and mentors **Time:** 1 hour	
5-9	**Assessment Planning Matrix** **Purpose:** To plan the types of assessments for the activities, lessons and skills taught in a specific unit of study. **Materials:** Unit plans **Who:** Mentee and mentor individual or as partners **Time:** 2 hours	

MONTH FIVE

ACTIVITY 5-1

EXAMINING ASSESSMENT HISTORY

Directions: Answer the following questions regarding your assessment history. Complete the questions independently and share the results with your learning partner or small group.

1. Describe a time in your life when assessment made you feel good about yourself as a learner.

2. Describe a time in your life when assessment did not make you feel good about yourself as a learner.

3. As a student, what types of assessment have helped you be successful?

4. As a student, what types of assessment do you find most challenging?

5. How has your experience with assessment as a student affected your assessment strategies as a teacher?

ACTIVITY 5-2

ASSESSMENT LITERACY INVENTORY

Directions: Both mentor and mentee complete the following literacy assessment rubric independently, then share it with each other. Review your ratings, and determine what areas you would like to focus on to improve your assessment literacy. Then complete the action plan on the next page.

	1 Need Assistance	2 Have Some Knowledge	3 Am Very Knowledgeable	Remarks:
1. I have a clear vision of my assessments before I introduce the lesson or unit with my students.				
2. I communicate about assessment goals with my students.				
3. Assessment goals are communicated in language my students understand.				
4. I communicate assessment results with parents.				
5. I use a variety of assessment strategies in my classroom instruction.				
6. I can easily identify which of my students need additional help.				
7. I know what types of extra help specific students need to succeed and achieve.				
8. My assessment strategies serve as tools to motivate my students to learn.				
9. I know how to match the skills outcome to the appropriate assessment method.				
10. I know which standards and skills are assessed on state assessments.				
11. I am knowledgeable about the state and/or local standardized tests that are administered in my school.				
12. I use rubrics to clarify assessment criteria.				
13. I understand the report card system in the district.				
14. I use assessment results to inform my instruction.				
15. I conference with my students and share information regarding their progress.				
16. My assessments clearly align with content, skills, and standards.				

Plan of Action

Directions: As you review the Assessment Literacy Inventory, identify specific areas you need to work on and list them below.

Area which needs further attention:	The plan to address identified assessment issues. (Include how the mentor/mentee learning partnership will help you.)	Follow-up date:

ACTIVITY 5-3

ANALYZING BEST ASSESSMENT METHODS

Directions: Identify a lesson or unit of study. Then describe the subject matter content and skills to be mastered by your students as a result of this lesson or unit, and the standards it is aligned with. Use the assessment methodology chart on the following page to help you.

Lesson or unit of study: _____

Achievement Targets: Subject matter content/skills	Standard(s):	Appropriate Assessment Method

ACTIVITY 5-3

ANALYZING BEST ASSESSMENT METHODS

Assessment Method Achievement Target	Selected Response • Multiple choice • True/false • Matching	Constructed Response	Performance Assessment	Observation Recording student conversations and discussions	Personal Communication
Mastery of Subject Matter, Knowledge and/or Specific Skill	Yes, especially appropriate for assessing baseline or foundation knowledge	Yes	Limited effectiveness; can assess mastery of subject matter to some extent	Yes, but limited due to time consuming nature of this assessment strategy	Yes, but time consuming; documentation must be included
Reasoning and Higher Order Thinking Skills	No	Yes, especially appropriate when rubrics are used	Yes	Yes, but limited due to time consuming nature of this assessment strategy	Yes, when asking students to solve problems verbally or explain reasoning
Performance and/or Product Development Skills	Limited effectiveness; this method only assesses pre-requisite skills, not performance	Limited effectiveness	Yes	Yes, but limited due to time consuming nature of this assessment strategy	Yes, when listening and speaking are part of the performance

ACTIVITY 5-4

ANALYZING WHOLE CLASS WORK

Directions: Each teacher gathers one set of graded assignments and brings them to share with his/her partner or small group. Analyze the assignments by filling out the chart below.

Describe the assignment:
Describe the desired learning targets:
Describe the way it was graded or scored:
Describe how the assessment did or did not assess the desired teaching and learning targets appropriately:
Describe how the overall class results help you determine if your class has a good understanding of the skills and concepts taught:
Describe what you learned from this activity. Share with your learning partner(s) and include your thoughts in your *Weekly Teacher Reflection Journal.*

ACTIVITY 5-4

INDIVIDUAL STUDENT ASSESSMENT ANALYSIS

Directions: Choose three students, one who performed well on the assignment, one who demonstrated average performance, and one who performed poorly. Analyze the individual student results and complete the following chart.

	Student Whose Performance was of Poor Quality	Student Whose Performance was of Average Quality	Student Whose Performance was of High Quality
What skill or understanding is evident in the completed assignment?			
How might the results be misinterpreted?			
Do you believe this is the best type of assessment for this student? Why or why not?			
What type of feedback would you offer this student?			
What did you learn about each student as a result of this assessment? Were there any surprises?			
If this is not the best type of assessment, what would be a better choice?			

Share and discuss your analysis of class and individual assessment results. How might these results cause you to modify this assignment? Record the results of your discussion below:

_____

_____

_____

_____

_____

_____

_____

_____

_____

_____

MONTH FIVE

ACTIVITY 5-5

CONSTRUCTED RESPONSE ACTIVITY

Constructed response assessment items are timed (usually 15 minutes), student-developed, written replies to a predetermined prompt. They are scored using a rubric that identifies different levels of proficiency. The constructed response has two scores, one for the communications component, and one for the content component.

DIRECTIONS: You and your partner will each complete the following constructed response. When you are finished, exchange papers with your partner and assess each other's work using the scoring rubric below. This activity is also suitable for small groups.

<u>Constructed Response Item</u>

Content Area: Language Arts   Topic: Merit Pay for Teachers

Thinking Skills: Generating Ideas, Analysis

Prompt: Your school district is considering a merit pay system for teachers. The School Board has asked you for your opinion of the proposal. Write a short paper (one or two paragraphs) stating at least two reasons why this is or is not a good idea. Support your argument with sound reasoning.

Constructed Response Scoring Rubric				
	Minimal – 1	**Basic - 2**	**Proficient - 3**	**Advanced - 4**
Communications	• Does not use correct paragraph format • Does not show logical order or focus • Sentences are not complete and well-developed • Many spelling, capitalization, and punctuation errors	• Has some difficulty using correct paragraph format • Has some difficulty with logical order and focus • Some sentences are complete and well-developed • Some spelling, capitalization, and punctuation errors	• Uses correct paragraph format • Maintains good logical order and focus • Sentences are complete and well-developed • Almost free of spelling, capitalization, and punctuation errors	• Uses correct paragraph format • Maintains exceptional logical order and focus • Sentences are complete and very well-developed • Free of spelling, capitalization and punctuation errors
Content Specific	• Does not state two reasons to support opinion • Does not develop argument	• States two reasons to support opinion • Does not develop argument for opinions	• States two reasons for opinion • Develops argument for both opinions reasonably well	• States more than two reasons • Develops argument for opinions very well

ACTIVITY 5-5

GUIDELINES FOR DEVELOPING CONSTRUCTED RESPONSE ITEMS

Along with your partner, design a constructed response item. Use the following guidelines:

- The prompt asks students for information related to content, story, or unit of study.
- The prompt asks students to respond to a scenario, question, dilemma, photo, diagram, story, chart, etc.
- The prompt asks students to use higher order thinking skills: gathering information, organizing information, generating ideas, synthesizing outcomes, and evaluating elements.
- Constructed response items are assessed using rubrics. A variety of sample rubrics is included.

Use the following template to help you:

MONTH FIVE

Constructed Response Template

Grade:_____ Content Area:_____ Topic:_____

State Performance Standard:

Thinking Skills:

Prompt:

Adapted from the constructed response model developed by the School district of Janesville, Wisconsin.

HOLISTIC SCORING GUIDE

First Grade

To be used with the Constructed Response Activity

	Minimal - 1	Basic - 2	Proficient - 3	Advanced - 4
Communications	**First Semester:** • Uses letters to communicate meaning **Second Semester:** • Spelling is based on sounds • Sentences don't make sense • Doesn't use capital letters and punctuation correctly	• Moves left to right • Uses letters to stand for sounds • Spells some words but most are based on sounds • Sentences are not always clear and complete • Sometimes uses capital letters and punctuation correctly	• Uses words to communicate meaning • Puts words together to tell ideas • Most words are spelled correctly • Sentences are clear and complete • Most of the time uses capital letters and punctuation correctly	• Words are spelled correctly • Beginning to use capital letters and periods • Words are spelled correctly • Sentences are clear, complete and have details • Punctuation and capital letters are correct.
Content Specific				

Note: The content specific boxes are to be completed by the teacher and should reflect levels of achievement of the constructed response topic.

HOLISTIC SCORING GUIDE

Second Grade

To be used with the Constructed Response Activity

	Minimal - 1	Basic - 2	Proficient - 3	Advanced - 4
Communications	• Sentences don't make sense • Ideas are not organized • Many errors in punctuation and capitalization • Spelling mostly based on sounds	• Sentences are not clear and complete • Ideas are not organized • Some errors in punctuation and capitalization • Some words are spelled correctly	• Sentences are clear and complete • Ideas are organized • Most punctuation and capitalization are correct • Most words are spelled correctly	• Sentences are clear and complete and include details • Ideas are well organized and show many things about this topic • Punctuation and capitalization are correct • Words are spelled correctly
Content Specific				

Note: The content specific boxes are to be completed by the teacher and should reflect levels of achievement of the constructed response topic.

HOLISTIC SCORING GUIDE

Grades 3-5

To be used with the Constructed Response Activity

	Minimal - 1	Basic - 2	Proficient - 3	Advanced - 4
Communications	• Many incorrect or incomplete sentences • Little or no organization of ideas • Errors in capitalization, punctuation, and spelling which interfere with meaning • Does not use correct paragraph structure	• Most sentences are complete • Some organization of ideas • Several errors in capitalization, punctuation and spelling • Attempts to use correct paragraph structure	• Sentences are complete • Ideas are organized • Capitalization, punctuation, and spelling almost free of errors • Uses correct paragraph structure	• Sentences are complete, well-developed and varied • Ideas are well organized • Capitalization, punctuation, and spelling are free of errors • Uses smoothly-flowing paragraphs with correct structure
Content Specific				

Note: The content specific boxes are to be completed by the teacher and should reflect levels of achievement of the constructed response topic.

HOLISTIC SCORING GUIDE

Middle and High School

To be used with the Constructed Response Activity

	Minimal - 1	Basic - 2	Proficient - 3	Advanced - 4
Communications	• Does not use correct paragraph format • Does not show logical order or focus • Sentences are not complete and well-developed • Vocabulary is not appropriate to grade level • Many spelling, capitalization, and punctuation errors	• Sometimes uses correct paragraph format • Has some difficulty with logical order and focus • Some sentences are complete and well-developed • Vocabulary is appropriate to grade level • Some spelling, capitalization, and punctuation errors	• Almost always uses correct paragraph format • Typically maintains logical order and focus • Sentences are complete and well-developed • Vocabulary is appropriate to grade level • Almost free of spelling, capitalization, and punctuation errors	• Always uses correct paragraph format • Maintains logical order and focus • Sentences are complete and well-developed • Vocabulary exceeds expectations of grade level • Free of spelling, capitalization and punctuation errors
Content Specific				

Note: The content specific boxes are to be completed by the teacher and should reflect levels of achievement of the constructed response topic.

ACTIVITY 5-6

USING WRITING RUBRICS TO ASSESS STUDENT WRITING SAMPLES

Rubrics describe different degrees of quality or levels of proficiency based on academic standards. Rubrics provide consistent scoring and feedback for teachers and students. Clearly written rubrics also allow students to self-monitor their work and provide learning expectations before and during the assignment for all stakeholders.

Directions: Bring 4-6 ungraded student writing samples to the seminar. Using the writing rubrics provided, assess the student writing samples by checking the appropriate boxes that most closely describe the qualities presented on the writing sample. When you have completed assessing your writing samples discuss the following questions with your learning partner(s).

1. What were the advantages of using the provided writing rubrics to assess your writing samples?

2. In what ways did this exercise help you understand your students' writing ability?

3. What are the challenges associated with using a rubric to assess student writing?

4. How would you implement a writing rubric in your classroom practice?

RUBRICS

Writing Rubric: Grades 1.5-2

Name _____   Title _____   Date _____

	Content Specific – examples, creativity, originality	Organization – paragraph structure, details, etc.	Language Use – descriptive words, vocabulary, etc.	Mechanics – capitalization, punctuation, etc.	Spelling
Advanced – 4	❑ Writing sample has clearly defined beginning, middle and end ❑ Topic is developed in an interesting and imaginative way	❑ Always shows organization of events ❑ Always uses supporting details	❑ Always demonstrates subject/verb agreement ❑ Ideas are always stated clearly ❑ Always uses descriptive vocabulary	❑ Always uses appropriate capital letters and punctuation ❑ Always uses complete sentences ❑ Always uses neat handwriting	❑ No spelling errors on priority words
Proficient – 3	❑ Writing sample almost always has clearly defined beginning, middle, and end ❑ Topic is developed with little imagination	❑ Almost always shows organization of events ❑ Almost always uses supporting details	❑ Almost always demonstrates subject/verb agreement ❑ Ideas are almost always stated clearly ❑ Uses some descriptive vocabulary	❑ Almost always uses appropriate capital letters and punctuation ❑ Almost always uses complete sentences (minimal fragments and run-ons) ❑ Almost always uses neat handwriting	❑ Almost always spells priority words correctly (1-2 errors)
Basic – 2	❑ Writing sample sometimes has clearly defined beginning, middle and end ❑ Attempts to develop the topic but digresses	❑ Sometimes shows organization of events ❑ Sometimes uses supporting details	❑ Sometimes demonstrates subject/verb agreement ❑ Ideas are sometimes stated clearly ❑ Uses little descriptive vocabulary	❑ Sometimes uses appropriate capital letters and punctuation ❑ Sometimes uses complete sentences (some fragments and run-ons) ❑ Sometimes uses neat handwriting	❑ Some priority words spelled incorrectly (3-5 errors)
Minimal – 1	❑ Writing sample seldom has clearly defined beginning, middle and end ❑ Minimally addresses the topic	❑ Seldom uses organization of events ❑ Seldom uses supporting details	❑ Seldom demonstrates subject/verb agreement ❑ Ideas are seldom stated clearly ❑ Uses no descriptive vocabulary	❑ Seldom uses appropriate capital letters and punctuation ❑ Seldom uses complete sentences (many fragments and run-ons) ❑ Seldom uses neat handwriting	❑ Many priority words spelled incorrectly (more than 5)

Adapted from rubrics developed by the school district of Lake Geneva, Wisconsin.

MONTH FIVE

RUBRICS

Writing Rubric: Grades 3-5

Name _____ Title _____ Date _____

	Content Specific – examples, creativity, originality	Organization – paragraph structure, details, etc.	Language Use – descriptive words, vocabulary, etc.	Mechanics – capitalization, punctuation, etc.	Spelling
Advanced – 4	□ More than adequately develops topic □ Always appropriate to purpose	□ Always uses logical order □ Always uses proper paragraph structure	□ Always uses specific and descriptive vocabulary □ Always uses complete sentences □ Always uses appropriate tense □ Always uses correct subject/verb agreement □ Always uses clear and varied sentence structure	□ Always uses appropriate capital letters Exceeds expectations of presentation (appearance) □ Always uses appropriate punctuation	□ No spelling errors
Proficient – 3	□ Adequately develops topic □ Almost always appropriate to purpose	□ Almost always uses logical order □ Almost always uses proper paragraph structure	□ Almost always uses specific and descriptive vocabulary □ Almost always uses complete sentences □ Almost always uses appropriate tense □ Almost always uses correct subject/verb agreement □ Almost always uses clear and varied sentence structure	□ Almost always uses appropriate capital letters Meets expectations of presentation (appearance) □ Almost always uses appropriate punctuation	□ Almost always uses correct spelling (1-2 errors)
Basic – 2	□ Attempts to develop topic □ Sometimes appropriate to purpose	□ Sometimes uses logical order □ Sometimes uses proper paragraph structure	□ Sometimes uses specific and descriptive vocabulary □ Sometimes uses complete sentences □ Sometimes uses appropriate tense □ Sometimes uses correct subject/verb agreement □ Sometimes uses clear and varied sentence structure	□ Sometimes uses appropriate capital letters Meets some expectations of presentation (appearance) □ Sometimes uses appropriate punctuation	□ Some words spelled incorrectly (3-5 errors)
Minimal – 1	□ Does not develop topic □ Seldom appropriate to purpose	□ Seldom uses logical order □ Seldom uses proper paragraph structure	□ Seldom uses specific and descriptive vocabulary □ Seldom uses complete sentences □ Seldom uses appropriate tense □ Seldom uses correct subject/verb agreement □ Seldom uses clear and varied sentence structure	□ Seldom uses appropriate capital letters □ Does not meet expectations of presentation (appearance) □ Seldom uses appropriate punctuation	□ Many words spelled incorrectly (more than 5)

Adapted from rubrics developed by the school district of Lake Geneva, Wisconsin.

RUBRICS

Writing Rubric: Middle School

Name _____   Title _____   Date _____

	Content Specific – examples, creativity, originality	Organization – paragraph structure, details, etc.	Language Use – descriptive words, vocabulary, etc.	Mechanics – capitalization, punctuation, etc.
Advanced – 4	☐ Always appropriate to purpose of assignment ☐ Always exhibits voice ☐ Always cites references correctly when required	☐ Always demonstrates paragraphing skills (topic sentence, sufficient support details, closing sentence) ☐ Always demonstrates logical order ☐ Always uses effective transitions ☐ Always maintains focus	☐ Word choice always appropriate to context ☐ Always uses effective sentence structure ☐ Excellent use of figurative language (when appropriate) ☐ Always uses sentence variety ☐ Always uses appropriate tense	☐ No spelling, capitalization, punctuation errors
Proficient – 3	☐ Almost always appropriate to purpose of assignment ☐ Almost always exhibits voice ☐ Almost always cites references correctly when required	☐ Almost always demonstrates paragraphing skills (topic sentence, sufficient support details, closing sentence) ☐ Almost always demonstrates logical order ☐ Almost always uses effective transitions ☐ Almost always maintains focus	☐ Word choice almost always appropriate to context ☐ Almost always uses effective sentence structure ☐ Uses figurative language (when appropriate) ☐ Almost always uses sentence variety ☐ Almost always uses appropriate tense	☐ Few spelling, capitalization, punctuation errors
Basic – 2	☐ Sometimes appropriate to purpose of assignment ☐ Sometimes exhibits voice ☐ Sometimes cites references correctly when required	☐ Sometimes demonstrates paragraphing skills (topic sentence, sufficient support details, closing sentence) ☐ Sometimes demonstrates logical order ☐ Sometimes uses effective transitions ☐ Sometimes maintains focus	☐ Word choice sometimes appropriate to context ☐ Sometimes uses effective sentence structure ☐ Sometimes uses figurative language (when appropriate) ☐ Sometimes uses sentence variety ☐ Sometimes uses appropriate tense	☐ Some spelling, capitalization, punctuation errors
Minimal – 1	☐ Seldom appropriate to purpose of assignment ☐ Seldom exhibits voice ☐ Does not cite references correctly when required	☐ Seldom demonstrates paragraphing skills (topic sentence, sufficient support details, closing sentence) ☐ Seldom demonstrates logical order ☐ Seldom uses transitions ☐ Seldom maintains focus	☐ Word choice is not appropriate to context ☐ Seldom uses effective sentence structure (some fragments and run-ons) ☐ Does not use figurative language (when appropriate) ☐ Seldom uses sentence variety ☐ Seldom uses appropriate tense	☐ Many spelling, capitalization, punctuation errors

Adapted from rubrics developed by the school district of Lake Geneva, Wisconsin.

MONTH FIVE

RUBRICS

Writing Rubric: High School

Name _____ Title _____ Date _____

	Content Specific – examples, creativity, originality	Organization – paragraph structure, details, etc.	Language Use – descriptive words, vocabulary, etc.	Mechanics – capitalization, punctuation, etc.
Advanced – 4	☐ Ideas are always appropriate to the purpose ☐ Ideas always demonstrate understanding of context ☐ Ideas are always well reasoned ☐ Ideas always combine original thought and classroom content ☐ When assigned, sources are always referenced/cited	☐ Always uses effective transitions ☐ Always uses topic sentences ☐ Always puts ideas in a logical order ☐ Always supports ideas with appropriate examples and details	☐ Vocabulary always appropriate to context ☐ Always uses effective sentence structure ☐ Always uses descriptive language ☐ Always uses sentence variety	☐ No spelling errors ☐ Always uses correct capitalization ☐ Always uses correct punctuation ☐ Always uses correct subject/verb agreement ☐ Always uses correct tense agreement
Proficient – 3	☐ Ideas are almost always appropriate to the purpose ☐ Ideas almost always demonstrate understanding of context ☐ Ideas are almost always well reasoned ☐ Ideas almost always combine original thought and classroom content ☐ When assigned, sources are almost always referenced/cited	☐ Almost always uses effective transitions ☐ Almost always uses topic sentences ☐ Almost always puts ideas in a logical order ☐ Almost always supports ideas with appropriate examples and details	☐ Vocabulary almost always appropriate to context ☐ Almost always uses effective sentence structure ☐ Almost always uses descriptive language effectively ☐ Almost always uses sentence variety	☐ Nearly free of spelling errors ☐ Almost always uses correct capitalization ☐ Almost always uses correct punctuation ☐ Almost always uses correct subject/verb agreement ☐ Almost always uses correct tense agreement
Basic – 2	☐ Ideas are sometimes appropriate to the purpose ☐ Ideas sometimes demonstrate understanding of context ☐ Ideas are sometimes well reasoned ☐ Ideas sometimes combine original thought and classroom content ☐ When assigned, sources are sometimes referenced/cited	☐ Sometimes uses effective transitions ☐ Sometimes uses topic sentences ☐ Sometimes puts ideas in a logical order ☐ Sometimes supports ideas with appropriate examples and details	☐ Vocabulary sometimes appropriate to context ☐ Sometimes uses effective sentence structure ☐ Sometimes uses some descriptive language ☐ Sometimes uses sentence variety	☐ Numerous spelling errors ☐ Sometimes uses correct capitalization ☐ Sometimes uses correct punctuation ☐ Sometimes uses correct subject/verb agreement ☐ Sometimes uses correct tense agreement
Minimal – 1	☐ Ideas are seldom appropriate to the purpose ☐ Ideas seldom demonstrate understanding of context ☐ Ideas are seldom well reasoned ☐ Ideas seldom combine original thought and classroom content ☐ When assigned, sources are seldom referenced/cited	☐ Seldom uses effective transitions ☐ Seldom uses topic sentences ☐ Seldom puts ideas in a logical order ☐ Seldom supports ideas with appropriate examples and details	☐ Vocabulary seldom appropriate to context ☐ Seldom uses effective sentence structure ☐ Seldom uses descriptive language ☐ Seldom uses sentence variety	☐ Numerous spelling errors ☐ Seldom uses correct capitalization ☐ Seldom uses correct punctuation ☐ Seldom uses correct subject/verb agreement ☐ Seldom uses correct tense agreement

Adapted from rubrics developed by the school district of Lake Geneva, Wisconsin.

ACTIVITY 5-7

EXAMINING DISTRICT AND/OR STATE STANDARDIZED ASSESSMENTS

Directions: Local and state standardized exams are a reality in nearly every school district. What do you know about the current standardized assessment methods administered in your district? Answer the following questions to help you better understand your local system and how students in your district perform on those assessments.

1. What standardized exams are administered to the students in your district? Are they mandated by the state, district, or both?
2. What content areas are assessed?
3. At what grade levels are the assessments administered?
4. When are the standardized exams administered?
5. How are the results shared with teaching staff?
6. How are the results shared with parents?
7. How are the results shared with the public?
8. How are the results used? Do they result in changes in curriculum, teaching practice, or modifications for individual students?
9. In what ways are the results of mandated exams important to your teaching practice?
10. Are measurable goals set for the district as a result of analyzed standardized assessment data?

ACTIVITY 5-8

GRADING ISSUES:
GIVING STUDENTS THE GRADES THEY DESERVE

Directions: The table below illustrates the assessment results of four students. The quarter grades were based on the percentage of total points each student earned. Each student received a 79% – a grade of C – for the semester.

Examine the table and with your learning partner or small groups discuss the questions following the table.

Assessment	Point Value	Student One	Student Two	Student Three	Student Four
Homework	10	9	3	4	10
Quiz	25	16	24	10	23
Exam	100	69	95	68	90
Homework	10	10	4	0	9
Project	50	48	25	30	45
Homework	5	5	0	4	4
Homework	5	5	0	4	4
Quiz	25	15	24	23	21
Homework	5	5	2	5	3
Exam	75	57	73	73	64
Project	40	37	25	37	25
Homework	10	9	3	9	5
Exam	50	30	47	48	22
Total	410	315	325	315	325
Extra Credit		10	------	10	----
Total	410	325	325	325	325
Percentage		79%	79%	79%	79%
Grade		C	C	C	C

Grading Scale: 90% - 100% = A
80%- 89%   = B
70% - 79%   = C
60% - 69%   = D
Below 60%   = F

Additional information about the students:

Student One is a very outgoing and hard-working student. She is very involved in many activities and has very good leadership skills. She misses class only when she has a student council commitment or choir rehearsal due to special programs.

Student Two is a very capable young man who tends to be argumentative and disruptive in class. He rarely misses class.

Student Three is new to the district and tends to be quiet, contributing only when directly asked. Her attendance was rather inconsistent at the beginning of the quarter but more recently has been very good.

Student Four missed a significant number of class periods toward the end of the semester. When he was in class, he sometimes participated in class discussion, but only when asked.

Based on their grades and descriptions, what conclusions might you draw about each student?

_____

_____

_____

_____

Do you believe each of these students deserve a grade of C?

_____

_____

_____

_____

What other types of assessment could be included to give us a better picture of the achievement of these four students?

_____

_____

_____

_____

What types of interventions would you plan to help these students raise their grades?

_____

_____

_____

_____

MONTH FIVE

Activity 5-9

ASSESSMENT PLANNING MATRIX

Directions: Complete the following chart to help you plan your assessments. Share the plan with your learning partner(s).

Activity/Lesson/ Skill ➡️ How You Plan to Assess Student Thinking/ Achievement ⬇️								
Teacher-made selected response exam								
Teacher-made constructed response items								
Textbook tests								
Teacher observation								
Journals								
Essays								
District writing assessment								
Classroom writing assignments								
Interviews								
Performance-based projects								
State writing assessment								
Critical incidents								
State mandated standardized tests								
District standardized tests								

REQUIRED FORMS SECTION

Monthly Seminar Planning Form

Partners use this form to select which monthly activities each would like to focus on at the monthly seminar. The coordinator collects this form and plans the seminars based on the feedback of participants.

Weekly Teacher Reflection Journal (duplicate as needed)

Each partner completes this form at the end of the week by taking 10 – 15 minutes to answer the reflection prompts. The weekly sheets are saved and used to complete the *Monthly Reflection Journal Summary*.

Monthly Reflection Journal Summary

Each partner completes this form prior to the monthly seminar meeting. The summary is used for dialogue and discussion with partners or groups. This sheet is saved every month.

Monthly Support Seminar Evaluation

Participants complete this form after the monthly support seminars. The coordinator collects and keeps these for ongoing assessment and revision of the mentor program.

MONTHLY SEMINAR PLANNING FORM

Date _____

Mentor Name _____

Mentee Name _____

Monthly Seminar Topic _____

I have reviewed this month's suggested activities and would like to focus on the following partner or small group activity:

Activity Number_____

Title _____

Mentee or Mentor Name _____

WEEKLY TEACHER REFLECTION JOURNAL

(Duplicate as needed)

Name: Date:

1. When did I feel the most connected, engaged, or affirmed as a teacher this week, especially regarding assessment? When did I feel most confident and competent with my assessment skills?

2. When did I feel the most disconnected, disengaged, or discouraged as a teacher this week, especially regarding assessment? When did I doubt my assessment competence and confidence?

3. If I could repeat this week, what would I do differently based on the learning and responses of my students, especially regarding assessment?

4. What am I most proud of this week based on the learning and responses of my students? Were there particular successes related to assessment?

5. Other thoughts about this week:

MONTHLY REFLECTION JOURNAL SUMMARY

Understanding Assessment

Directions: Look at your current and past responses to the prompts in your weekly reflection journal. Use a highlighter to find themes or patterns to your responses about each question. Summarize your entries under each of the prompts. Save this sheet!

1.   Summarize the situations where you felt the most connected, engaged, or affirmed as a teacher this month especially about assessment issues. Summarize the times you felt most confident and competent with your assessment skills.

Connected, Engaged, Affirmed	Confident and Competent with Assessment Skills

2.   Summarize the situations where you felt the most disconnected, disengaged, or discouraged as a teacher this month especially about assessment issues. Summarize when you doubted your competence and confidence, especially about assessment skills.

Disconnected, Disengaged, Discouraged	Not Confident and Competent with Assessment Skills

3.   Summarize what you would do differently based on student learning and responses for the month, especially regarding assessment issues.

Student Learning and Responses	What I'd Do Differently

4.   Summarize what you are most proud of this month based on student learning and responses. Were there particular successes related to assessment?

Student Learning and Responses	What I'm most proud of

**MONTHLY SUPPORT SEMINAR EVALUATION
MONTH/TOPIC:**

1. List the activity you chose to focus on this month:

2. List the learning partner(s) you worked with to complete this activity:

3. What was the most important thing you learned about this month's topic?

4. How has this month's activity influenced your classroom teaching?

5. What other monthly activities included in this chapter do you plan to complete?

6. What data will you collect as a result of this month's activity?

7. What suggestions do you have for improving the monthly seminars?

Month Six

CONTENT STANDARDS AND CURRICULUM

*It's not enough to do your best; you must know what to do
and then do your best.*

W. Edwards Deming

INTRODUCTION TO MONTH SIX

Student academic standards and curriculum define what subject matter students should be taught and when they should encounter it. Behind this simple definition, however, is an extremely challenging process. Standards can be numerous and difficult to interpret; curriculum is often an outdated, fragmented intermixture of textbooks, district guidelines, and the personal preference of the teacher. It is often up to the classroom teacher to bridge the gap between standards and curriculum. It's a tough job, and in this age of accountability the stakes are high. Failure to support the standards (and the assessments tied to them) results in poor student performance that will have negative consequences for students, faculties, and schools.

On the bright side, integrating standards into daily teaching is a creative task that demands that teachers be informed, thoughtful, and active participants in making the standards come to life through an engaging, up-to-date, and meaningful curriculum. It's also an excellent opportunity for teachers to work as colleagues, sharing the load and learning from each other's experiences. To be successful in enhancing student learning, this collaborative work must be founded on a good understanding of the standards, a well-developed curriculum that reflects the daily reality of the classroom, and a clear vision of how the two are connected.

The activities presented this month help teachers understand and analyze standards and curriculum issues by focusing on these essential questions:

1. What are the standards and benchmarks (i.e., the student learning expectations) for my grade level?

2. What is the curriculum for my grade level and other grade levels?

3. Does the curriculum align with the academic standards?

4. Do I know the standards that precede and follow my grade level?

Both mentees and mentors should begin with Activity 6-1, a self-assessment that will help them identify their basic knowledge about standards and curriculum. This self-assessment leads to the development of an action plan for further work and learning on these topics.

Activities 6-2 and 6-3 give partners an opportunity to analyze standards, revise them to become more "user-friendly," and identify those standards that are essential. By *essential*, we mean those standards on which most emphasis will be placed at your particular subject or grade level.

Activity 6-4 helps the partners identify *meaningful* curriculum. Curriculum use should be meaningful in the sense that it prepares teachers to provide the kind of instruction that will help students meet the learning expectations expressed in state or district standards.

CONTENT STANDARDS

Most states across the nation have standards that describe what students should know and be able to do throughout the grades. The standards provide guidelines for district curriculum development and instruction that lead to the goal of successful student learning and achievement.

A state or district typically has two types of standards. *Content standards* are broad curricular expectations of the material students should know and be able to do. For example, a content standard from Wisconsin's Model Academic Standards reads: *Students will read and respond to a wide range of writing to build an understanding of written materials, themselves, and of others.*

In addition to content standards, states and districts develop statements that describe specific learning expectations at specific grade levels (1st, 2nd, and 3rd, for example) or groups of grade levels. These descriptions often are called *performance standards* or *benchmarks*. Regardless of their name, the focus is on the specific learning that must be accomplished by a designated time. For example, the Wisconsin Reading Content Standard above has this performance standard:

By the end of grade four students will:
- *Use effective reading strategies to achieve their purposes in reading*
- *Read, interpret, and critically analyze literature*
- *Read and discuss literary and non literary texts in order to understand human experience*
- *Read to acquire information*

MONTH SIX

CURRICULUM

While standards typically come from a single source – a state education department, a national professional organization, or a school district – the curriculum itself may have numerous sources. In many districts, teachers representing specific content areas form committees to write the district's curriculum in that subject. These content-specific committees usually meet to write and revise the curriculum in three- to five-year cycles. Curriculum can also be based on the scope and sequence of specific textbooks, teacher-made materials, supplemental materials, and the personal preferences of teachers. With all these curriculum sources, it is no wonder that the outcome is often disjointed and can foster inconsistent instruction that results in uneven student achievement. It is important for new teachers to have an understanding of the district curriculum, how and where it is articulated, where it came from, and whether it aligns with state or district content standards.

LEARNING TARGETS

- Develop a good understanding of the standards and benchmarks.

- Understand that standards must be interpreted to provide clear, usable guidance for all stakeholders.

- Understand that standards provide the structure from which the local curriculum is created.

- Understand that classroom teaching must be clearly aligned with academic standards.

- Know who is responsible for teaching and assessing which standards, and when.

RESOURCES

Carr, J., & Harris, D. (2001). *Succeeding with standards: Linking curriculum, assessment, and action planning.* Alexandria, VA: Association for Supervision and Curriculum Development.

Erickson, L. (1998). *Concept-based curriculum and instruction.* Thousand Oaks, CA: Corwin Press.

Erickson, L. (1995). *Stirring the head, heart and soul.* Thousand Oaks, CA: Corwin Press.

Jacobs, H. H. (1997). *Mapping the big picture.* Alexandria, VA: Association for Supervision and Curriculum Development.

Reeves, D. (2001). *Standards are not enough: Essential transformation for successful schools.* Keynote presentation at the National School Conference Institute, Las Vegas, NV.

Reeves, D. (1998). *Making standards work.* Boston, MA: Center for Performance Assessment.

Rogers, S., & Graham, S. (1998). *The high performance toolbox.* Evergreen, CO: Peak Learning Systems.

Sargent, J., & Smejkal, A. (2000). *Targets for teachers: A self study guide for teachers in the age of standards.* Winnepeg, Canada: Portage & Main.

Strong, R., Silver, H., & Perini, M. (2001). *Teaching what matters most: Standards and strategies for raising student achievement.* Alexandria, VA: Association for Supervision and Curriculum Development

Wisconsin Department of Public Instruction (1998). *Wisconsin's model academic standards.* Wisconsin Department of Public Instruction.

MONTH SIX

MONTH SIX SUPPORT SEMINAR ACTIVITIES

Number	Activity	Date Completed
	REQUIRED ACTIVITIES • Monthly Seminar Planning Form • Weekly Teacher Reflection Journal • Monthly Reflection Journal Summary • Monthly Support Seminar Evaluation	
6-1	**Standards and Curriculum Questionnaire** **Purpose:** To help the mentee and mentor determine their knowledge of standards and curriculum. **Materials:** Activity worksheet 6-1 **Who:** Mentor and mentee each complete Part One independently and then share the results with each other. **Time:** 60 minutes (20 minutes to complete and 40 minutes for sharing and developing action plan).	
6-2	**Standards Analysis** **Purpose:** To understand and analyze the standards. **Materials:** Activity worksheet 6-2, State Content Standards **Who:** Mentor and mentee learning partners **Time:** 60 minutes	
6-3	**Identifying and Focusing on Essential Standards** **Purpose:** To identify the essential standards based on established criteria. **Materials:** Activity worksheet 6-3, State Content Standards **Who:** Mentor and mentee learning partners and/or small groups **Time:** 90 minutes	
6-4	**What Is Useful Curriculum?** **Purpose:** To learn what makes curriculum useful for teachers, students and parents and use these criteria to determine the usefulness of the curriculum the partners currently use. **Materials:** Activity worksheet 6-4 **Who:** Mentor/mentee learning partners and/or small groups **Time:** 90 minutes	

ACTIVITY 6-1

STANDARDS AND CURRICULUM QUESTIONNAIRE

Directions: Both mentor and mentee complete the following questionnaire and share it with each other. Based on your ratings, determine which areas you would like to focus on to improve your knowledge of standards and curriculum.

	1 Yes	2 Yes, somewhat	3 I need help	Remarks:
1. The content standards are clearly posted and visible in my classroom.				
2. I am very familiar with the standards at my grade level.				
3. I know which standards are assessed on the standardized tests administered in my district.				
4. The academic standards we use are presented in a way that is easily understood and useable for teachers, students, and parents.				
5. I have a good understanding of the curriculum for my grade level or the course I am teaching.				
6. I have analyzed and identified the standards for what my students must know and be able to do.				
7. The curriculum that guides my teaching is based on a clearly defined purpose.				
8. The curriculum that guides my teaching is clearly aligned with academic standards.				
9. I know the curriculum content and skills that precede and follow the grade level or course I am teaching.				
10. I have enough time and opportunity to discuss curriculum issues with my colleagues.				
11. The parents and students in my classroom have a clear vision of what students are expected to know and be able to do.				

Plan of Action

As you review the standards and curriculum questionnaire, what specific areas do you need to work on? Please list them below.

Area which needs further attention:	My plan:	Follow-up date:

ACTIVITY 6-2

STANDARDS ANALYSIS

Many standards are written in language that is difficult to understand, let alone figure out how to teach. Making the standards more "user-friendly" involves analyzing and interpreting what basic understanding the standard requires, describing how it will be implemented and assessed, and stating it in clear, concise language. This activity provides a process for this analysis and rewriting.

Directions: With your learning partner, choose a content standard and analyze it by answering the following questions.

Choose a content standard and write it here:
What skills will students need to meet this standard?
What resources will you need to teach this standard?
What content area(s) does this standard encompass?
How will you assess how well your students meet the learning expectations in this standard?
What other standard(s) does this standard overlap with?
How do the learning expectations in this standard connect to students' lives?
How would you rewrite this standard in more user-friendly language?

ACTIVITY 6-3

IDENTIFYING AND FOCUSING ON ESSENTIAL STANDARDS

Content standards can be complicated and unclear. In some states the standards are vague and difficult to understand; in others, the standards are so numerous that it is nearly impossible to teach them all in a K-12 school system. Use the following criteria suggested by Reeves (2001) to assist you in identifying those standards on which you and your students will place the most emphasis:

1. The standards that have stood the test of time and those that teachers, who are the experts in their respective fields, know are important;

2. The standards that have application in other disciplines;

3. The standards that are prerequisites for the next level of instruction;

4. The standards that are assessed on the mandated standardized assessments.

This activity will provide an opportunity to identify and focus on the essential standards.

Directions: Choose a content standard and its related performance standards or benchmarks. Discuss in small groups or with your learning partner the extent to which the particular standard meets the listed criteria. It will be impossible in the time allocated to complete this activity for all the standards in your state or district. However, you can use this same process any time you need to make decisions about which standards are truly essential.

Standard	This standard can stand the test of time	This standard has application in other disciplines	This standard is a pre-requisite for the next level of instruction	This standard is assessed on the mandated standardized assessment

ACTIVITY 6-4

WHAT IS USEFUL CURRICULUM?
Nearly every district has some type of formal curriculum that is designed to guide instruction. These guides are usually comprised of large binders that are often too cumbersome and outdated to be useful in classroom instruction. It has been our experience that most teachers rarely refer to these guides. Instead, they rely on textbooks, supplemental materials, and their personal preference to guide their instruction. In the fragmented curriculum that often results, some important material may go untaught, while other material is repeated needlessly. To be meaningful and useful for meeting student needs, the curriculum must be an accessible tool that effectively guides instruction and is aligned both to standards and the curriculum of other grade levels.

Directions: Consider the curriculum you currently use to guide your instruction and compare it to the criteria listed in the chart below.

The following curriculum sources guide my instruction (please list):

_____

_____

Considering the curriculum sources you listed above, complete the following chart:

Criteria The curriculum I currently use to guide instruction is:	Yes	Somewhat	No	We Need:
Highly visible and accessible to teachers, students, and parents				
Presented in a user-friendly format				
Easily and continually revised on a timely basis, based on teacher input, collaboration, and the latest research				

A tool that is easy for teachers new to the district to use				
A tool that provides information about the skills that precede and follow a particular grade level or course				
At the core of teaching practice				
Clearly aligned with standards				
Your additions:				

Based on your analysis of the curriculum you currently use to guide instruction, what key areas need further attention to meet the needs of all students more effectively?

_____

_____

_____

_____

_____

What are the specific steps you would take to create a more useful curriculum?

_____

_____

_____

_____

_____

REQUIRED FORMS SECTION

Monthly Seminar Planning Form

Partners use this form to select which monthly activities each would like to focus on at the monthly seminar. The coordinator collects this form and plans the seminars based on the feedback of participants.

Weekly Teacher Reflection Journal (duplicate as needed)

Each partner completes this form at the end of the week by taking 10 – 15 minutes to answer the reflection prompts. The weekly sheets are saved and used to complete the *Monthly Reflection Journal Summary*.

Monthly Reflection Journal Summary

Each partner completes this form prior to the monthly seminar meeting. The summary is used for dialogue and discussion with partners or groups. This sheet is saved every month.

Monthly Support Seminar Evaluation

Participants complete this form after the monthly support seminars. The coordinator collects and keeps these for ongoing assessment and revision of the mentor program.

MONTHLY SEMINAR PLANNING FORM

Date _____

Mentor Name _____

Mentee Name _____

Monthly Seminar Topic _____

I have reviewed this month's suggested activities and would like to focus on the following partner or small group activity:

Activity Number _____

Title _____

Mentee or Mentor Name _____

WEEKLY TEACHER REFLECTION JOURNAL

(Duplicate as needed)

Name: Date:

1. When did I feel the most connected, engaged, or affirmed as a teacher this week, especially regarding standards and curriculum? When did I feel most confident and competent with my standards and curriculum skills?

2. When did I feel the most disconnected, disengaged, or discouraged as a teacher this week, especially regarding standards and curriculum? When did I doubt my standards and curriculum competence and confidence?

3. If I could repeat this week, what would I do differently based on the learning and responses of my students, especially regarding standards and curriculum?

4. What am I most proud of this week based on the learning and responses of my students? Were there particular successes related to standards and curriculum?

5. Other thoughts about this week:

MONTHLY REFLECTION JOURNAL SUMMARY

Analysis of Standards and Curriculum

Directions: Look at your current and past responses to the prompts in your weekly reflection journal. Use a highlighter to find themes or patterns to your responses about each question. Summarize your entries under each of the prompts. Save this sheet!

1. Summarize the situations where you felt the most connected, engaged, or affirmed as a teacher this month, especially about standards and curriculum issues. Summarize the times you felt most confident and competent with your standards and curriculum skills.

Connected, Engaged, Affirmed	Confident and Competent with Standards and Curriculum Skills

2. Summarize the situations where you felt the most disconnected, disengaged, or discouraged as a teacher this month, especially about standards and curriculum issues. Summarize when you doubted your competence and confidence especially in the areas of standards and curriculum.

Disconnected, Disengaged, Discouraged	Not Confident and Competent With Standards and curriculum Skills

3. Summarize what you would do differently based on student learning and responses for the month, especially about standards and curriculum.

Student Learning and Responses	What I'd Do Differently

4. Summarize what you are most proud of this month based on student learning and responses. Were there particular successes related to standards and curriculum?

Student Learning and Responses	What I'm most proud of

MONTHLY SUPPORT SEMINAR EVALUATION
MONTH/TOPIC:

1. List the activity you chose to focus on this month:

2. List the learning partner(s) you worked with to complete this activity:

3. What was the most important thing you learned about this month's topic?

4. How has this month's activity influenced your classroom teaching?

5. What other monthly activities included in this chapter do you plan to complete?

6. What data will you collect as a result of this month's activity?

7. What suggestions do you have for improving the monthly seminars?

Month Seven

INSTRUCTIONAL METHODS

What I hear, I forget
What I hear and see, I remember a little.
What I hear, see and ask questions about or discuss with someone else, I begin to understand.
What I hear, see, discuss, and do, I acquire knowledge and skill.
What I teach to another, I master.
Mel Silberman

INTRODUCTION TO MONTH SEVEN

Months Five and Six focused on effective assessment strategies, standards, and curriculum, the "what" of teaching. This month, the partners use the foundational work from previous months to focus on methods for delivering the content – the "how" of teaching.

Teaching is not merely a series of fun activities; rather, it is a combination of meaningful and varied instructional strategies that emphasize academic standards and curriculum. To engage students and help them master content, teachers need to understand how students learn best and to incorporate that understanding into their lessons.

A well-crafted lesson, however, is only the first step to effective instruction. All teachers, especially those new to the profession, need to receive meaningful feedback about their classroom teaching practice. Giving and receiving feedback based on real classroom observation data can help both partners, the observer and the observed, improve their teaching performance. Throughout the first months of the mentor program, participants have been building a community of learners around the reciprocal, trusting partnership between mentor and mentee. In Month Seven, the learning partners will put this trusting relationship to the test by visiting each other's classrooms and giving each other meaningful, non-threatening feedback based on their observations.

Incorporating the latest research about student learning, this month's activities target the key elements of effective lesson plans and invite partners to analyze their own lessons in light of these factors. We also provide guidelines for positive, productive, reciprocal classroom visits. Each activity promotes reflection and conversation around these essential questions:

1. How do my students learn best?

2. How can I create student-centered lessons that focus on standards and curriculum and that include meaningful assessments?

3. How can I provide my partner with meaningful, non-threatening feedback when I visit his or her classroom?

KEY COMPONENTS OF LESSON DESIGN

What are the elements of effective teaching? A growing body of research suggests that students learn best in environments that are student-centered, active and experiential, collaborative, and reflective (Darling-Hammond, 1998; DuFour, 1998; Harmin, 1994; Sargent & Smejkal, 2000; Silberman, 1996).

For teachers, however, designing lessons and units that promote all these factors can be a challenging and complex process. Often, teachers tend to rely on strategies that reflect their own personal learning style. While it's natural for anyone to want to stay in his or her comfort zone, teachers must recognize that strategies that appeal to only one or two styles of learning will be ineffective for many students.

Understanding the complexities associated with creating effective lessons is essential for new teachers – and for veteran teachers as well. Both learning partners have knowledge and expertise to share with each other as they analyze and plan lessons. It is important for all teachers to examine the components of effective student learning and to create lessons, or modify existing lessons, to incorporate strategies that result in more effective instruction for all types of learners. Activity 7-1 provides an opportunity to analyze current lessons and plan for future lessons or units of study incorporating these student learning components:

Student Learning Components	Strategies
Student Centered A student-centered classroom creates learning experiences based on a student's real interests, concerns, and needs. It also considers a student's race, culture and gender. It is an environment that respects all learning styles and backgrounds, and accommodates the individual student with varied instructional practices.	• Give students choices • Incorporate multiple intelligences • Listen to student stories and questions • Plan lessons according to the age and development of students • Learn about student backgrounds and personal histories
Active/Experiential Students learn best by studying ideas, solving problems, discussing, debating, hypothesizing, investigating, and applying what they have learned.	• Connect content to real world • Involve guest speakers • Provide experiences that require students to sort, count, collect and analyze data, estimate, conduct experiments, take field trips, prepare reports, role-play • Connect new knowledge to prior learning

Student Learning Components	Strategies
Collaborative Students need opportunities to work together in cooperative ways. Students learn from each other when teamwork, collegiality, and mutual respect are encouraged.	• Use flexible grouping strategies: whole group, small groups, individual • Cooperative groups • Learning centers • Peer assessment • Group discussions • Peer tutoring
Reflective Provide verbal and written opportunities for students to debrief, discuss, and share their feelings about what they are learning.	• Students respond to written and verbal prompts • Journal writing • Self-assessment • Student conferences • Students share portfolios with peers and parents • Student learning logs

CLASSROOM VISITS

Our work with mentoring programs has shown us that some of the most important learning activities – and the most difficult to implement – are classroom visits. To improve their practice, all teachers need an image of what good teaching is. When we learn any new skill – golf, tennis, a musical instrument – we need more than instruction and practice. We also need to see the skill demonstrated and to demonstrate the skill ourselves to a knowledgeable coach who can give us feedback for improvement. No one argues with this concept, yet when teachers actually are faced with the reality of participating in classroom visits, there can be great resistance. Because most teachers' experience with classroom visits is associated with formal teaching supervision and evaluation, the very thought of being observed can cause anxiety, even in an informal setting with a well-meaning colleague looking on.

One of the goals of this mentor program is to foster an atmosphere of trust and mutual support that can overcome this hesitation and encourage both the mentor and mentee to participate in non-threatening classroom visits with the intention of shared learning and growth. When novice teachers receive feedback from knowledgeable colleagues, mistakes can be corrected before they become major problems, positive behaviors can be reinforced, and effective teaching behaviors can be developed (Podsen & Denmark, 2000). By the same token, novice teachers can also serve as important resources for veteran teachers. New teachers may know more about recently developed instructional strategies and may have used them in student teaching. Especially in the sciences, a new teacher may also have more current knowledge than a colleague who has been teaching for a number of years (Stansbury & Zimmerman, 2001). The feedback and learning in mutual classroom visits is truly a two-way street.

Activity 7-2 provides a step-by-step guide for successful classroom visits. These visits should be completed *before* the monthly support seminar, in which participants will discuss the outcomes of the classroom visits. We strongly encourage the learning partners to participate in at least one classroom visit.

LEARNING TARGETS

- Understand that lesson plans and units of study must maintain a tight focus on the big ideas or essential understandings for that topic.

- Incorporate strategies that reflect how students learn best into lessons and units of study.

- Understand and experience the benefits of participating in classroom visits.

MONTH SEVEN

RESOURCES

Campbell, B. (1994). *The multiple intelligences handbook.* Stanwood, WA: Campbell & Associates

Darling-Hammond, L. (1998). Teacher learning that supports student learning. *Educational Leadership,* 55 (5) 6-11.

Harmin, M. (1994). *Inspiring active learning.* Alexandria, VA: Association for Supervision and Curriculum Development.

Fogarty, R., & Stoehr, J. (1995). *Integrating curricula with multiple intelligences.* Palentine, IL: Skylight.

Perkins, D. (1999). The many faces of constructivism. *Educational Leadership* 57(3), 6-11.

Podsen, I., & Denmark, V. (2000). *Coaching and mentoring.* Larchmont, NY: Eye on Education.

Sargent, J., & Smejkal, A. (2000). *Targets for teachers: A self study guide for teachers in the age of standards.* Winnepeg, Canada: Portage & Main.

Silberman, M. (1996). *Active learning.* Boston: Allyn and Bacon.

Stansbury, K., & Zimmerman, J. (2001). Lifelines to the Classroom: Designing support for beginning teachers. *West Ed. Knowledge Brief.* San Francisco: West Ed.

Wiggins, G., & McTighe, J. (1998). *Understanding by design.* Alexandria, VA: Association for Supervision and Curriculum Development.

MONTH SEVEN SUPPORT SEMINAR ACTIVITIES

Number	Activity	Date Completed
	REQUIRED ACTIVITIES • Monthly Seminar Planning Form • Weekly Teacher Reflection Journal • Monthly Reflection Journal Summary • Monthly Support Seminar Evaluation	
7-1	**Writing An Effective Lesson or Unit** **Purpose:** To develop a lesson plan that includes essential components and strategies for optimum student learning. **Materials:** Existing lesson plan and/or lesson plan idea, current curriculum, standards document, and activity 7-1 lesson plan template **Who:** Mentor and mentee learning partners **Time:** 1.5 – 2 hours	
7-2	**Classroom Visits REQUIRED** *The pre-visit conference and the visit are to be completed before the monthly seminar.* **Purpose:** To observe each other in the classroom as learning partners, and to give and receive meaningful feedback. **Materials:** Pre-conference and post-conference templates, notes from classroom visit. **Who:** Mentor/mentee learning partners **Time:** 1 – 1.5 hours	

MONTH SEVEN

ACTIVITY 7-1

WRITING AN EFFECTIVE LESSON OR UNIT

Directions: Below are the components of an effective lesson or unit of study. With your mentoring partner, develop a lesson or modify an existing lesson based on these research-based components. Use the template on the next page to develop your lesson or unit.

Components of an Effective Lesson

Title, Content Area, Grade Level, Timeframe: The title, content area(s), the grade level and the projected time frame of the lesson or unit of study.

Standards and Benchmarks: Include the local or state standards and benchmarks that are the focus of this lesson or unit of study.

Enduring Concepts or Big Ideas: What are the enduring concepts or big ideas of this lesson or unit that you want your students to really know and be able to do? Ask yourself, "What is at the core of this lesson or unit?"

Teaching Strategies: These are the "delivery methods" that help students learn and apply essential understandings in order to meet performance benchmarks. These strategies must encourage a student-centered, active and experiential, collaborative, and reflective learning environment. You must decide how you will prepare your students to learn, how to motivate them, and how to conclude the lesson. Finally, the lesson should address the learning styles and other needs of your students.

Resources: What books, curricular materials, media, technology, or other resources will you need to implement this lesson or unit of study?

Assessment Plan: How will you know if and when students have met the learning targets? These assessment expectations must be clearly defined at the beginning of the lesson or unit and shared openly with students. Try to build in ongoing assessment strategies throughout the unit to monitor student progress. How will you intervene with students who are not learning the content? As with instruction, assessments must be balanced to best meet the needs of your students.

Next Steps: Be sure to define how this lesson connects to future lessons.

LESSON PLAN FORMAT

Title:

Grade Level and Content Area:

Timeframe:

Standards and Benchmarks:

Enduring Concepts/Big Ideas:

Activities:

Timeframe:

Teaching Strategies (strategies that help student meet the learning targets: student-centered, active/experiential, collaborative, reflective):

Resources (include guest speakers, technology, media, books, etc.)

Assessment Plan:

ACTIVITY 7-2

CLASSROOM VISITS

Directions: Using the form on page 150, the mentor and mentee will visit each other's classroom to observe each other teach. The purpose of the visits is to provide each other with meaningful feedback to enhance your teaching performance. Complete Part One and Part Two prior to the monthly seminar; you will complete Part Three during the seminar.

Part One: The Pre-conference or Pre-visit

Prior to the classroom visit, the learning partners meet to discuss the details of the visit. These details include the time of the visit, the goal or focus of the lesson, and a brief description of the lesson. This is also a good time for the partner who will be observed to share anything in particular the observing partner should pay specific attention to.

Part Two: The Visit

During the visit, the observing partner should take notes that are specific, descriptive, and nonjudgmental. It is very important to record only what you see and hear. The notes should be detailed enough to provide meaningful feedback to your learning partner.

Example of nonspecific feedback: *Brian did a great job teaching this lesson.*
This type of statement does not give Brian feedback that will help him identify what he was doing well and what areas might need improvement.

Example of specific feedback: *Using your musical talents to begin the lesson was a great strategy to get your kids' attention. Your students were immediately engaged. If we can work out the scheduling I would like you to demonstrate the African drumming to my students.*

Transitioning from large group to small group work went very well. Although it seemed to me that some students might have been confused about the directions, it flowed very well. If you are interested I can give you a handout regarding giving effective directions that I have found helpful.

The small group activities were very interesting and reflect our curriculum. It might have been a bit challenging for Jason's group, as they seemed to have a difficult time getting focused. I'm not sure you could see that from where you were in the classroom. It might help to make some modifications for them.

This type of feedback is much more meaningful because it provides detailed observations and suggestions for improving teaching practice.

Part Three: The Post-Visit or Post-Conference

An integral part of the classroom visit, the post conference is a time to look at the observation notes and other data together as true learning partners. It is vital that the post-conference occur soon after the visit. The following are questions that may guide your discussion:

- How do you think the lesson went?

- Why do you think it went that way?

- Were there any surprises?

- If you could teach this lesson again, what, if anything, would you do differently? Why?

- What conclusions can you draw from the way the lesson went?

CLASSROOM VISIT PLANNING AND IMPLEMENTATION TOOL

Part One: Pre-Visit Planning Conference

Date and time of the visit: _____

Length of visit: _____

The goal of the lesson will be: _____

_____

Brief description of the lesson: _____

_____

_____

_____

Particular things to watch for: _____

_____

_____

_____

Part Two: Classroom Visit Notes
The notes should be specific, descriptive, and nonjudgmental.

_____

_____

_____

_____

_____

_____

_____

Part Three: Post-Visit Conference

Use the observation notes and the following questions to guide the post-conference discussion.

How do you think the lesson went?

_____

_____

_____

Why do you think it went that way?

_____

_____

_____

Were there any surprises?

_____

_____

_____

If you could teach this lesson again, what, if anything would you do differently? Why?

_____

_____

_____

What conclusions can you draw from the way the lesson went?

_____

_____

As the observer I learned the following:

_____

_____

REQUIRED FORMS SECTION

Monthly Seminar Planning Form
Partners use this form to select which monthly activities each would like to focus on at the monthly seminar. The coordinator collects this form and plans the seminars based on the feedback of participants.

Weekly Teacher Reflection Journal (duplicate as needed)
Each partner completes this form at the end of the week by taking 10 – 15 minutes to answer the reflection prompts. The weekly sheets are saved and used to complete the *Monthly Reflection Journal Summary*.

Monthly Reflection Journal Summary
Each partner completes this form prior to the monthly seminar meeting. The summary is used for dialogue and discussion with partners or groups. This sheet is saved every month.

Monthly Support Seminar Evaluation
Participants complete this form after the monthly support seminars. The coordinator collects and keeps these for ongoing assessment and revision of the mentor program.

MONTHLY SEMINAR PLANNING FORM

Date _____

Mentor Name _____

Mentee Name _____

Monthly Seminar Topic _____

I have reviewed this month's suggested activities and would like to focus on the following partner or small group activity:

Activity Number _____

Title _____

Mentee or Mentor Name _____

WEEKLY TEACHER REFLECTION JOURNAL

(Duplicate as needed)

   Name: Date:

1. When did I feel the most connected, engaged, or affirmed as a teacher this week, especially regarding instructional methods? When did I feel most confident and competent with my instruction skills?

2. When did I feel the most disconnected, disengaged, or discouraged as a teacher this week, especially regarding instructional methods? When did I doubt my instruction competence and confidence?

3. If I could repeat this week, what would I do differently based on the learning and responses of my students, especially regarding instructional methods?

4. What am I most proud of this week based on the learning and responses of my students? Were there particular successes related to instructional methods?

5. Other thoughts about this week:

6. What were the most important things I learned while observing my learning partner's classroom?

7. What were the most important things I learned from my learning partner's feedback?

MONTHLY REFLECTION JOURNAL SUMMARY

Instructional Methods

Directions: Look at your current and past responses to the prompts in your weekly reflection journal. Use a highlighter to find themes or patterns in your responses to each question. Summarize your entries under each of the prompts. Save this sheet!

1. Summarize the situations where you felt the most connected, engaged, or affirmed as a teacher this month, especially about instructional methods. Summarize the times you felt the most confident and competent with your instructional methods.

Connected, Engaged, Affirmed	Confident and Competent with Skills

2. Summarize the situations where you felt the most disconnected, disengaged, or discouraged as a teacher this month, especially about instructional methods. Summarize when you doubted your competence and confidence, especially in the areas of instructional methods.

Disconnected, Disengaged, Discouraged	Not Confident and Competent with Skills

3. Summarize what you would do differently based on student learning and responses for the month, especially about instructional methods.

Student Learning and Responses	What I'd Do Differently

4. Summarize what you are most proud of this month based on student learning and responses. Were there particular successes related to instructional methods?

Student Learning and Responses	What I'm most proud of

**MONTHLY SUPPORT SEMINAR EVALUATION
MONTH/TOPIC:**

1. List the activity you chose to focus on this month:

2. List the learning partner(s) you worked with to complete this activity:

3. What was the most important thing you learned about this month's topic?

4. How has this month's activity influenced your classroom teaching?

5. What other monthly activities included in this chapter do you plan to complete?

6. What data will you collect as a result of this month's activity?

7. What suggestions do you have for improving the monthly seminars?

Month Eight

SETTING GOALS

An effective goal focuses primarily on results rather than on activity.
It defines where you want to be . . . and it tells you when you have arrived.
It unifies your efforts and energies.

Stephen Covey

INTRODUCTION TO MONTH EIGHT

Throughout the previous months' work, the learning partners have purposefully, collaboratively, and systematically collected and analyzed data related to their teaching practice. This month, both the mentor and mentee will review and synthesize the analyzed data and set appropriate learning goals for themselves that reflect their data analysis.

The data sources can include:

- *Weekly Teacher Reflection Journal*
- *Monthly Reflection Journal Summary*
- Support seminar activity worksheets
- Support seminar evaluations
- Classroom visit feedback
- Learning partner and small group conversations
- Other relevant teaching data

We present three activities this month; it is important that each activity be completed in the order presented. It may be too ambitious to complete all three activities during the time allotted for the monthly support seminar, so we encourage the learning partners to complete some work prior to the seminar. All three activities must be completed prior to Month Nine, at which time the learning partners will create a professional development plan based on the goals they identify.

The first activity asks the learning partners to analyze the data each has collected throughout the school year, determine areas of strength and concern, and identify the data that support these determinations. Activity 8-2 presents a goal setting matrix similar to that used in group goal-setting activities (Holcomb, 1999). Using the matrix, each learning partner identifies and rates the improvement areas that are of greatest concern, those that are of most immediate need, and those that can be accomplished in the timeliest manner. Based on the results, the teacher will identify one goal that is his or her greatest priority for professional improvement.

The last activity involves writing the goal using the SMART goals framework. This framework is widely used in government, business, and consulting; most recently, it has been adapted to be used in various education settings (O'Neill, 2000). The work of Garmston (1999) and DuFour (2001) provides two such examples and is the basis for our use of the SMART goals framework in these goal-setting activities. This framework asks the learning partners to examine their goals and indicate the extent to which the goals are specific, measurable, achievable, relevant, and tactically sound. The chart following describes each SMART goal criteria.

SMART GOALS FRAMEWORK

S	Specific Standards-Based	• Clearly focused on what is to be accomplished and why this is important • Based on standards for good teaching, which may include NBPTS, INTASC, individual state standards • Based on *what* must be accomplished, not *how* it is to be accomplished. The "how" will be the focus of the Professional Development Plan.
M	Measurable	• Must entail identifiable evidence of achievement • Must be based on results
A	Achievable	• Must be attainable within the time frame and resources available – must be within reach
R	Relevant	• Must address clear evidence of need based on multiple sources of data • Must be based on increased student learning. *How will meeting this goal help students?*
T	Tactically Sound	• Must identify the barriers and challenges in the process of meeting this goal. *Is it possible to overcome these barriers in the process of meeting this goal?*

The partners should concentrate on developing goals based on *what* they plan to accomplish, rather than detailing strategies for accomplishing the goal.

LEARNING TARGETS

- Analyze data gathered throughout the year related to classroom practice.

- Identify strengths and weaknesses of teaching practice.

- Set a specific, measurable, attainable, relevant and tactically sound goal based on analyzed data.

RESOURCES

Arhar, J., Holly, M., & Kasten, W. (2001). *Action research for teachers*. Columbus, OH: Merrill Prentice Hall.

Covey, S. (1989). *The seven habits of highly effective people*. New York: Simon & Schuster.

Danielson, C., & McGreal, T. (2000). *Teacher evaluation: To enhance professional practice*. Alexandria, VA: Association for Curriculum and Supervision.

DuFour, R., & Burnette, B. (2001). *Building professional learning communities*. Presentation at the Wisconsin State Reading Association, Milwaukee, WI, August 3, 2001.

Garmston, R. & Wellman, B. (1999). *The adaptive school: A sourcebook for developing collaborative groups*. Norwood, MA: Christopher-Gordon Publishers, Inc.

Holcomb, E. (1999*). Getting excited about data*. Thousand Oaks, CA: Corwin Press, Inc.

O'Neill, J. (2000). SMART goals, SMART schools. *Educational Leadership*, *57* (5) 46-50.

Richardson, J. (February/March, 2002). Reach for the stars: Individual learning plans allow teacher to take charge of their own learning. *Tools for Schools*. Oxford, OH: National Staff Development Council

Schmoker, M. (1996). *Results.* Alexandria, VA: Association for Curriculum and Supervision.

Schmoker, M. (2001). *The results fieldbook.* Alexandria,VA: Association for Curriculum and Supervision.

Walton, Mary (1986). *Demming management method*. New York: Perigee Books.

MONTH EIGHT SUPPORT SEMINAR ACTIVITIES

Number	Activity	Completed Date
	REQUIRED ACTIVITIES • Monthly Seminar Planning Form • Weekly Teacher Reflection Journal • Monthly Reflection Journal Summary • Monthly Support Seminar Evaluation	
8-1	**Analyzing Collected Data** **Purpose:** To examine all data that has been collected as a result of the mentor program activities and identifies areas of strengths and weaknesses. **Materials:** Activity worksheet 8-1, all data that have been collected throughout the year **Who:** All mentors and mentees work independently. *This activity can be completed before the monthly seminar.* **Time:** 45 minutes	
8-2	**Identifying Areas of Greatest Concern** **Purpose:** To prioritize the areas of greatest need, immediacy, and attainability, and then identify the focus area for writing the goal. This activity builds on Activity 8-1. **Materials:** Completed worksheet 8-1 and Activity worksheet 8-2 **Who:** Mentors and mentees work independently to complete the chart, then meet as partners to discuss the results. **Time:** 45 minutes	
8-3	**Writing a Goal Based on SMART Goal Criteria** **Purpose:** To write a goal based on the completion of Activity 8-2 and using the SMART Goal analysis sheet **Materials:** Activity worksheet 8-3 **Who:** Mentor and mentee working as partners **Time:** 1 hour	

ACTIVITY 8-1

ANALYZING COLLECTED DATA TO DETERMINE STRENGTHS
AND AREAS OF WEAKNESS

Directions: Using the data that you have collected throughout the year, identify your areas of strength and the areas that are in the greatest need of improvement. Include the data sources you used to determine these results.

Areas of Strengths	Data Sources	Areas in Need of Improvement	Data Sources

ACTIVITY 8-2

IDENTIFYING AREAS OF GREATEST CONCERN

Directions: Look at the areas of greatest concern you identified in Activity 8-1. Record those areas in the chart below. After each statement, use a five-point scale to rate the degree of need, the degree of immediacy, and the degree to which you believe you can meet the goal in a timely manner. When you have completed rating each area, add the total for each area in the far right column. The areas with the highest numbers are the areas of greatest concern, immediacy and "doability". Review your findings with your learning partner for feedback and discussion. When you are finished, record your proposed goal.

Area of Concern	Degree of Need Rate each item 1-5 5 = most important area of concern based on multiple and reoccurring data sources	Degree of Immediacy Rate each item 1-5 5 = most important area to be addressed as soon as possible	Degree of Attainability Rate each item 1-5 5 = most likely to be attained within a reasonable timeframe	Total Number

Based on the findings from the goal-setting matrix, the focus area for my goal is: _____

ACTIVITY 8-3

WRITING A GOAL BASED ON SMART GOAL CRITERIA

Directions: Complete the following SMART goals chart to determine if the goal is specific, measurable, achievable, relevant and tactically sound.

Use the completed chart on the following page to help you.

SMART GOALS FRAMEWORK

My proposed goal: _____

	SMART GOAL CRITERIA	HOW THE GOAL MEETS THE SMART GOAL CRITERIA
S	**Specific Standards-Based**	• Clearly focused on what is be accomplished and why this is important • Based on Standards for good teaching, which may include NBPTS, INTASC, or individual state standards • Based on *what* is to be accomplished, not *how* it is to be accomplished. The "how" will be the focus of the Professional Development Plan.	
M	**Measurable**	• Can this goal be measured? • Will I be able to identify evidence of achievement?	
A	**Achievable**	• Can this goal be attained within the timeframe and resources available? • Can I set a definite timetable to complete this goal?	
R	**Relevant**	• Is this goal based on multiple sources of data? • How will meeting this goal help students?	
T	**Tactically Sound**	• Will there be barriers and challenges in the process of meeting this goal? • How will I overcome these barriers and challenges?	

Discuss the results of the SMART Goals analysis with your learning partner, revise the goal as needed, and record the goal below. Your goal will become the focus of the Professional Development Plan you will develop in Month Nine.

My Goal: _____

ACTIVITY 8-3

WRITING A GOAL BASED ON SMART GOAL CRITERIA

Directions: Complete the following SMART goals chart to determine if the goal is specific, measurable, achievable, relevant and tactically sound.

SAMPLE

SMART GOALS FRAMEWORK

My proposed goal: *To learn and implement classroom management strategies to better engage my students to write and deliver speeches at a proficient level of achievement.*

	SMART GOAL CRITERIA	HOW THE GOAL MEETS THE SMART GOAL CRITERIA
S **Specific Standards-Based**	• Clearly focused on what is to be accomplished and why this is important. • Based on Standards for good teaching, which may include NBPTS, INTASC, or individual state standards. • Based on *what* is to be accomplished not *how* it is to be accomplished. The "how" will be the focus of the Professional Development Plan.	*Disruptive student behavior is interfering with my teaching and student learning.* *My students need to be attentive so they can learn to write and deliver speeches.* *This goal is based on teaching standards related to classroom management and student achievement.* *The goal clearly states what I hope to accomplish.*
M **Measurable**	• Can this goal be measured? • Will I be able to identify evidence of achievement?	*Yes, by having fewer office referrals for disruptive student behavior, and designing and using more effective assessment tools (i.e., rubrics) that clearly communicate and assess student achievement.*
A **Achievable**	• Can this goal be attained within the timeframe and resources available? • Can I set a definite timetable to complete this goal?	*Yes, there are multiple district resources available: district-wide courses in classroom management and assessment, professional library resources, and opportunities to observe and/or interview other expert teachers.* *This is my goal for the following semester and next school year.*
R **Relevant**	• Is this goal based on multiple sources of data? • How will meeting this goal help students?	*Yes, low student achievement, high incidence of disruptive student behavior, frustration of teacher and students, inconsistent or unclear learning expectations.* *Students will be better writers and oral communicators.*
T **Tactically Sound**	• Will there be barriers and challenges in the process of meeting this goal? • How will I overcome these barriers and challenges?	*The challenge will be to change existing (student and teacher) behavior but there are adequate learning opportunities and building support to help overcome this challenge.* *Learning new strategies for monitoring student behavior and communicating learning expectations more clearly.*

Discuss the results of the SMART Goals analysis with your learning partner, revise the goal as needed, and record the goal below. Your goal will become the focus of the Professional Development Plan you will develop in Month Nine.

My Goal: *To learn and implement classroom management strategies to better engage my students to write and deliver speeches at a proficient level of achievement.*

MONTH EIGHT

HOW THE GOAL MEETS THE SMART GOAL CRITERIA		
S	Specific Standards-Based	
M	Measurable	
A	Achievable	
R	Relevant	
T	Tactically Sound	

Discuss the results of the SMART Goals analysis with your learning partner, revise the goal as needed, and record the goal below. Your goal will become the focus of the Professional Development Plan you will develop in Month Nine.

My Goal:

_____
_____
_____
_____
_____
_____

REQUIRED FORMS SECTION

Monthly Seminar Planning Form

Partners use this form to select which monthly activities each would like to focus on at the monthly seminar. The coordinator collects this form and plans the seminars based on the feedback of participants.

Weekly Teacher Reflection Journal (duplicate as needed)

Each partner completes this form at the end of the week by taking 10 – 15 minutes to answer the reflection prompts. The weekly sheets are saved and used to complete the *Monthly Reflection Journal Summary*.

Monthly Reflection Journal Summary

Each partner completes this form prior to the monthly seminar meeting. The summary is used for dialogue and discussion with partners or groups. This sheet is saved every month.

Monthly Support Seminar Evaluation

Participants complete this form after the monthly support seminars. The coordinator collects and keeps these for ongoing assessment and revision of the mentor program.

MONTHLY SEMINAR PLANNING FORM

Date _____

Mentor Name _____

Mentee Name _____

Monthly Seminar Topic _____

I have reviewed this month's suggested activities and would like to focus on the following partner or small group activity:

Activity Number _____

Title _____

Mentee or Mentor Name _____

WEEKLY TEACHER REFLECTION JOURNAL

(Duplicate as needed)

Name: Date:

1. When did I feel the most connected, engaged, or affirmed as a teacher this week? When did I feel most confident and competent with my skills?

2. When did I feel the most disconnected, disengaged, or discouraged as a teacher this week? When did I doubt my competence and confidence?

3. If I could repeat this week, what would I do differently based on the learning and responses of my students?

4. What am I most proud of this week based on the learning and responses of my students?

5. Other thoughts about this week:

MONTHLY REFLECTION JOURNAL SUMMARY

Setting Goals

Directions: Look at your current and past responses to the prompts in your weekly reflection journal. Use a highlighter to find themes or patterns in your responses to each question. Summarize your entries under each of the prompts. Save this sheet!

1.   Summarize the situations where you felt the most connected, engaged, or affirmed as a teacher this month. Summarize times you felt the most confident and competent.

Connected, Engaged, Affirmed	Confident and Competent

2.   Summarize the situations where you felt the most disconnected, disengaged, or discouraged as a teacher this month. Summarize when you doubted your competence and confidence.

Disconnected, Disengaged, Discouraged	Not Confident and Competent

3.   Summarize what you would do differently based on student learning and responses for the month.

Student Learning and Responses	What I'd Do Differently

4.   Summarize what you are most proud of this month based on student learning and responses.

Student Learning and Responses	What I'm most proud of

MONTHLY SUPPORT SEMINAR EVALUATION
MONTH/TOPIC:

1. List the activity you chose to focus on this month:

2. List the learning partner(s) you worked with to complete this activity:

3. What was the most important thing you learned about this month's topic?

4. How has this month's activity influenced your classroom teaching?

5. What other monthly activities included in this chapter do you plan to complete?

6. What data will you collect as a result of this month's activity?

7. What suggestions do you have for improving the monthly seminars?

Month Nine

WRITING THE PROFESSIONAL DEVELOPMENT PLAN

"Would you tell me please which way I ought to walk from here?" asked Alice.
"That depends a good deal on where you want to get to," said the Cat.
Lewis Carroll

INTRODUCTION TO MONTH NINE

Adventures in teaching can seem as chaotic and confusing as those of Alice in Wonderland – unless teachers set goals for the skills and abilities they want to develop for themselves and then follow a coherent, step-by-step plan to reach them. The goals developed in Month Eight provide the compass that will direct the partners as they develop a professional growth plan. This plan, in turn, becomes the map that will guide their walk through the unknown territory of each school year, allowing them to correct their course as they learn along the way.

The plan should answer five basic questions (Holcomb, 1996):

1. Where do I want to go?
2. Where am I now?
3. How will I get there?
4. How will I know I am there?
5. What do I need to do next?

Many who have participated in a formal planning process before, and have seen it result in little actual change, may greet this effort with a degree of skepticism. After all, anything is possible on paper; in order to move off the paper and into reality, however, a professional growth plan must be *meaningful, manageable* and *measurable*.

The meaning comes from the teacher's desire to increase his or her own effectiveness. To be meaningful, the plan's goals and strategies must be grounded in a pattern of strengths and needs based on teacher perception and student feedback, as reflected in the *Weekly Teacher Reflection Journal*, the *Monthly Reflection Journal Summary,* and other data the partners have collected throughout the year. Based on those patterns, the teacher defines a plan that meets his or her needs and interests, all ultimately serving the primary objective of increased student learning. However lofty it may otherwise be, without the meaning provided by the teacher's own motivations for improvement, a goal will be unlikely to inspire the energies the teacher will need to attain it.

A plan also must be manageable to be successful. It must take into realistic account the time, resources, and effort required to complete it, and must balance those needs with all of the other demands the teacher must meet. The teacher must choose carefully the strategic steps that will help him or her gain the knowledge, skills, and dispositions needed to accomplish the goal. The selection process must focus on activities that will have the greatest impact on success and that can be balanced with the teacher's daily professional and personal activities. This requires a calibration of time, challenge, weekly reflection, and personal desire.

Just as data were important in defining professional development goals in Month Eight, measurement will yield the data that indicate whether the plan is on track. The effects of the activities on teacher knowledge, skills, and dispositions, as well as on student learning, must be carefully quantified so that benchmarks of success can be established. Professional development plans are often measured by the volume of teacher activity without corresponding measurements for results, especially those results that impact student behavior or achievement. Activity 9-1 provides an example of how to determine the kind of measurement that will provide useful evidence, either of progress or of the need to revise the plan.

The format for the Annual Professional Growth Plan chart presented in Month Nine contains the crucial components necessary to build a meaningful, manageable, and measurable plan:

1. Goal Statement:
This section answers the question, "Where do I want to go?" Participants have already developed this statement in Month Eight, using criteria for writing SMART goals. As such, the goal is a natural outgrowth of the professional's assessment of his or her strengths and needs, and is directly connected to standards for quality teaching.

2. Current Status:
This answers the question, "Where am I now?" This descriptive paragraph justifies the selection of the goal or goals, and is also based on the self-assessment work done in Month Eight. This description is important because it marks the starting point of the plan and is used as a comparative baseline to measure growth and progress toward the goal. It lets the planner know just how far he or she has come.

3. Action Steps:
The first two questions set up a creative tension that looks for resolution (Fritz, 1989). Action steps answer the third question, "How will I get there?" Action steps provide direction for attaining the goal and should be strategic so that their results incrementally narrow the gap between the current status and the goal.

Two points need to be emphasized about the action steps included in the plan. First, the steps must be selected wisely to meet the criteria of meaningfulness, manageability, and measurability. More is not better. Put into priority those activities that give you the most results for the effort.

Second, the activity itself is not as important as the actual impact that activity has on professional growth and student learning. For example, a course in classroom management is listed as the first Action Step on the Sample Plan (Activity 9-1). The course is a logical activity, given the planner's current status and goal. However, the course is NOT the result; it is a step towards the result. It provides a catalyst for the teacher to gain and apply information, monitor the effects on student learning, reflect, and determine what needs to happen next. This is why the *Weekly Teacher Reflection Journal* and the *Monthly Reflection Journal Summary* are also included as Action Steps, serving to keep the teacher focused on professional growth over time and the effects on student learning. Action Steps 3 through 5 are activities that build off the knowledge gained from the course and help the teacher know how she is doing and what effect her new strategies are having.

To select activities wisely, it is helpful to:

- Brainstorm the types of activities that would achieve the goal.
- Prioritize the activities, identifying those that are strategic and are the most doable.
- Consider the resources needed and the time required to complete the activity.
- Look for possible barriers that may prevent you from implementing the activities you selected, and see if there are ways to overcome the barriers. Some of these barriers may involve your access to resources and your ability to control circumstances. For example, Action Step 3 on the sample may be difficult to complete if scheduling does not allow for co-teaching. If our planner is aware of this difficulty in advance, she may be able to enlist the support of another teacher so that she can overcome this barrier.
- Select activities that provide the best movement toward the goal, those that will have the best chance of producing the professional growth and enhanced student learning you seek.

4. Resources Needed:

This is another aspect of "How will I get there?" This section describes the resources – help, time, budget, materials – essential for achieving the goals (see Sample Plan section IV). They must be available, affordable, and applicable to the Action Step.

5. Timelines:

Timelines are a crucial tool for managing the step-by-step achievement of the goal. A well-constructed timeline helps you plan to complete the Action Steps in the proper order and helps you spot potential conflicts or time crunches. Of course, things may not happen according to your schedule. In our Sample Plan, our teacher was forced to revise her timeline to adjust for the availability of a course she wanted to take (see V and VII).

However, her timeline did help her quickly see the impact of that change on her entire plan, and make other adjustments accordingly. As a result, she was able to change her schedule – instead of having to abandon her goal and activity. As much as possible, make sure the timelines are appropriate, and check ahead for dates and commitments to eliminate unforeseen consequences.

6. Evidence:

Evidence answers the fourth question, "How will I know I am there?" Covey (1992) writes that evaluation is both the final step of the plan, and the first step to a living and learning cycle. As we plan, act, evaluate our actions, and plan again, we repeat the cycle of learning and growth. Reflections and evidence collected along the way demonstrate our continuing progress toward our overall goals. Notice that our sample teacher has designated a variety of kinds of evidence – journal samples, witnessed accounts, written observations, video comparisons, student data, and so on – she will collect and use to document both professional growth and student learning results.

7. Revisions:

Revisions are included because plans are dynamic; they change along the way, either in light of changing circumstance or as a result of your learning and observations. A plan that is not continually revisited and revised quickly becomes irrelevant. Revisions keep the document alive, allowing you to be flexible about the details while maintaining a constant focus on your overall goal. The sample plan (section VII) illustrates how revisions are written when timelines change. In this case, the activity remained the same; only the timeframe changed. However, if the course was *not* offered, the plan might have to be revised to include a workshop, consultation with colleagues on getting strategies, reading, or some other way to gain knowledge about the subject.

8. Summary of the Evidence:

As the plan unfolds throughout the year, the teacher should collect evidence, in the form of written materials or artifacts, that illustrates the closing of the gap between the teacher's initial status and the desired goal. This is the same kind of documentary process the partners used in Month Eight to determine their strengths and needs. Focusing on the goal statement and the progress made during the year, the documentation of evidence substantiates the plan's effects on professional growth and effects on student learning. In our sample plan, videos, sample student lessons over time, and the use of the speech rubric, all serve to indicate how close the planner came to reaching the goal. As in most improvement models, analyzing results at the end of a plan marks the beginning of a new growth cycle. This becomes the "current status" on which teachers will base next year's professional development plan, continuing the cycle of learning and growth.

Professional development is a dynamic, active process that requires continued reflection on how one's teaching practice affects student learning. Therefore, we recommend that teachers continue to use the *Weekly Teacher Reflection Journal* and the *Monthly Reflection Journal Summary* during Year Two as they implement the growth plan. It will provide important evidence of the plan's effectiveness and point to necessary mid-course corrections as the plan unfolds.

Writing the professional growth plan is the only activity required this month. This plan will provide the direction that guides both mentor and mentee as they continue their partnership in the following year through reflection, collaboration, and focused attention on student learning.

LEARNING TARGETS

- Create a professional growth plan that is meaningful, measurable and manageable.
- Create a plan that promotes professional growth towards achieving standards of teaching excellence that have a positive effect on student learning.

RESOURCES

Brown, J. L., & Moffett, C. A. (1999). *The hero's journey: How educators can transform schools and improve learning.* Alexandria, VA: Association for Supervision and Curriculum Development.

Cochran-Smith, M., & Lytle, S. L. (1993). *Teacher research and knowledge.* New York: Teachers College Press.

Galpin, T. J. (1996). *The human side of change.* San Francisco: Jossey-Bass.

Fritz, R. (2001). *The path of least resistance video guide.* St. Paul, MN: Star Thrower Distribution Corporation.

Fritz, R. (1991). *Creating.* New York: Ballentine Books.

Fritz, R. (1989). *The path of least resistance.* New York: Ballentine Books

Fritz, R. (1985). *Creating what you always wanted to but couldn't believe before because nobody ever told you how because they didn't know either.* Salem, MA: DMA, Inc.

Garmston, R. (1999). *The adaptive school.* Norwood, MA: Christopher-Gordon Publishers.

Holcomb, E. (1996). *Asking the right questions.* Thousand Oaks, CA: Corwin Press, Inc.

Kessler, R. (2000). *The soul of education: Helping students find connection, compassion, and character at school.* Alexandria, VA: Association for Supervision and Curriculum Development.

Levine, S. (1999). *A passion for teaching.* Alexandria, VA: Association for Supervision and Curriculum Development.

National Research Council (2000). *How people learn.* Washington, D.C.: National Academy Press.

National Staff Development Council (Feb. 2001). Student work at the core of teacher learning. *Results.* Oxford, OH: National Staff Development Council.

National Staff Development Council (August/September 2001). Learning teams. *Tools for Schools.* Oxford, OH: National Staff Development Council.

Sher, B. (1979). *Wishcraft: How to get what you really want.* NewYork: Ballentine Books.

Speck, M., & Knipe. C. (2001). *Why can't we get it right: Professional development in our schools.* Thousand Oaks, CA: Corwin Press.

MONTH NINE SUPPORT SEMINAR ACTIVITIES

Number	Activity	Completed Date
	REQUIRED ACTIVITIES • Monthly Seminar Planning Form • Weekly Teacher Reflection Journal • Monthly Reflection Journal Summary • Monthly Support Seminar Evaluation	
9-1	**Reviewing the Professional Growth Plan (Sample)** **Purpose:** To become familiar with the components of a professional growth plan **Materials:** Activity worksheet 9-1 **Who:** Mentor and/or Mentee **Time:** 30 minutes or more for reading and discussion	
9-2	**Writing the Professional Growth Plan** **Purpose:** To develop a plan that promotes professional growth towards teacher standards of excellence and has a positive effect on student learning. **Materials:** Activity worksheet 9-2, reflection journal summaries and other entries, copy of resources if needed **Who:** Mentee, with or without the mentor's assistance **Time:** 1-2 hours (or more depending on knowledge of resources)	

ACTIVITY 9-1

REVIEWING THE PROFESSIONAL GROWTH PLAN (SAMPLE)

Name: Yesiama Lerner Position: Secondary English/Speech

Building: John Dewey High District: Excell, Illinois

Planning Cycle: Beginning Month/Year: August, 2002 Ending Month/Year: June, 2003

I.	Goal Statement:	(Where do I want to go?)

Goal Statement: To learn and implement classroom management strategies to better engage my students to write and deliver speeches at a proficient level of achievement.

Professional Teaching Standard/s Addressed:

Standard #5: The teacher uses an understanding of individual and group motivation and behavior to create a learning environment that encourages positive social interaction, active engagement in learning, and self motivation.

Standard #4: The teacher is a reflective practitioner who continually evaluates the effects of his/her choices and actions on others (students, parents and other professionals in the learning community) and who actively seeks out opportunities to grow professionally.

II.	Current Status:	(Where am I now?)

I often noted concerns about classroom discipline in my *Weekly Teacher Reflection Journal.* The first month I sent two students to the office for detentions for continuous talking. My mentor and I talked about classroom routines and the need to enforce rules consistently. By the end of the first quarter, I sent the two students to the office 10 times. Even with new students, the second semester was no improvement. I had 20 office detentions, this time by different students. I want to increase my skills in handling behavior that disrupts the classroom but I also want to engage the students in learning speech techniques and deliver good speeches. I could improve 1) my consistency in rules and routines; 2) my ability to motivate and engage ALL students and; 3) assist students to take charge of their own learning so that they can meet a high level of expectation in speech. I currently use a rubric to evaluate student speeches. The students who were most disruptive made little or no progress. Overall, I think all my students could have done better to improve the quality of their speeches if I managed the class better.

III. Action Steps (How will I get there?) (i.e., Study group, workshops, books, videos, serve on committee, peer coaching, college course, action research, conferences, learning partner, on-line network, etc.)	IV. Resources Needed (Time, money, or people)	V. Timeline for Completion (Estimate the time of completion for EACH activity. May modify in column VII.)	VI. Evidence Collected (How will I know I'm there?) (i.e., student work samples, video, etc.)	VII. Revisions Needed & Why
1. Take a summer course in classroom management at the university.	• Money for registration! (But I get reimbursed through my contract!)	June - July, 2002 Three week session.	• Successful completion of course. • Strategies I can plan to use when school starts	The course is only offered for 3 weeks in July...but offered first semester. I'm registered for the fall class on Monday nights.
2. Practice using the strategies and use the *Weekly Teacher Reflection Journal* to record reflections on how successful I am.	• Time for Weekly Reflection Journal (20 minutes/week)	August 2002 - June 2003	• Journal samples • Use to guide revisions of plan • Data collection & analysis	Revised to begin September 2002 because I don't have the strategies yet.
3. Have a colleague co-teach to demonstrate motivational strategies and give me tips to use.	• Colleague in the English Dept. or someone who will volunteer (may be special education)	October 2002 - February 2003	• Witness account of my skills • Document observations • Use rubric to assess quality	
4. Use video samples of my classes at the beginning, middle, and end of the year and critique my progress.	• Video-recorder • Technology support • Video tape • Parent permission (?)	September 2002 - June 2003	• Video comparison of student behavior with a written analysis • Use rubric to make teaching adjustments	
5. Use student problem-solving methods.	• Forms in Month Four	September 2002 - June 2003	• Student data and evaluation of problem-solving methods. • Connect to achievement	

ACTIVITY 9-2

WRITING THE PROFESSIONAL GROWTH PLAN

Name: Position:

Building: District:

Planning Cycle: Beginning Month/Year: Ending Month/Year:

I.   Goal Statement: (Where do I want to go?)
Goal Statement:
Professional Teaching Standard/s Addressed:
II.   Current Status: (Where am I now?)
Provide description of why you selected this goal. Make the justification as quantifiable as you can.

III. Action Steps (How will I get there?) (i.e., Study group, workshops, books, videos, serve on committee, peer coaching, college course, action research, conferences, learning partner, on-line network, etc.)	IV. Resources Needed (Time, money, or people)	V. Timeline for Completion (Estimate the time of completion for EACH activity. May modify in column VII.)	VI. Evidence Collected (How will I know I'm there?) (i.e., student work samples, video, etc.)	VII. Revisions Needed & Why

VIII. Summary of Evidence (Include materials & artifacts such as student work samples, before-and-after videos, presentation materials, summaries of reflection, etc.)	Effects on Teacher Professional Growth (What did I learn?)	Effects on Student Learning (What effect did this have on student learning?)

REQUIRED FORMS SECTION

Monthly Seminar Planning Form

Partners use this form to select which monthly activities each would like to focus on at the monthly seminar. The coordinator collects this form and plans the seminars based on the feedback of participants.

Weekly Teacher Reflection Journal (duplicate as needed)

Each partner completes this form at the end of the week by taking 10 – 15 minutes to answer the reflection prompts. The weekly sheets are saved and used to complete the *Monthly Reflection Journal Summary*.

Monthly Reflection Journal Summary

Each partner completes this form prior to the monthly seminar meeting. The summary is used for dialogue and discussion with partners or groups. This sheet is saved every month.

Monthly Support Seminar Evaluation

Participants complete this form after the monthly support seminars. The coordinator collects and keeps these for ongoing assessment and revision of the mentor program.

MONTHLY SEMINAR PLANNING FORM

Date _____

Mentor Name _____

Mentee Name _____

Monthly Seminar Topic _____

I have reviewed this month's suggested activities and would like to focus on the following partner or small group activity:

Activity Number _____

Title _____

Mentee or Mentor Name _____

WEEKLY TEACHER REFLECTION JOURNAL

(Duplicate as needed)

Name: Date:

1. When did I feel the most connected, engaged, or affirmed as a teacher this week? When did I feel most confident and competent with my skills?

2. When did I feel the most disconnected, disengaged, or discouraged as a teacher this week? When did I doubt my competence and confidence?

3. If I could repeat this week, what would I do differently based on the learning and response of my students?

4. What am I most proud of this week based on the learning and responses of my students?

5. Other thoughts about this week:

MONTHLY REFLECTION JOURNAL SUMMARY

Writing the Professional Development Plan

Directions: Look at your current and past responses to the prompts in your weekly reflection journal. Use a highlighter to find themes or patterns in your responses to each question. Summarize your entries under each of the prompts. Save this sheet!

1. Summarize the situations where you felt the most connected, engaged, or affirmed as a teacher this month. Summarize situations where you felt the most confident and competent.

Connected, Engaged, Affirmed	Confident and Competent with Skills

2. Summarize the situations where you felt the most disconnected, disengaged, or discouraged as a teacher this month. Summarize when you doubted your competence and confidence.

Disconnected, Disengaged, Discouraged	Not Confident and Competent with Skills

3. Summarize what you would do differently based on student learning and responses for the month.

Student Learning and Responses	What I'd Do Differently

4. Summarize what you are most proud of this month based on student learning and responses.

Student Learning and Responses	What I'm most proud of

MONTHLY SUPPORT SEMINAR EVALUATION
MONTH/TOPIC:

1. List the activity you chose to focus on this month:

2. List the learning partner(s) you worked with to complete this activity:

3. What was the most important thing you learned about this month's topic?

4. How has this month's activity influenced your classroom teaching?

5. What other monthly activities included in this chapter do you plan to complete?

6. What data will you collect as a result of this month's activity?

7. What suggestions do you have for improving the monthly seminars?

Month Ten and Beyond

The Cycle Continues:
Sustaining the Momentum

INTRODUCTION TO MONTH TEN AND BEYOND

The close of the mentoring cycle brings two related challenges. On one hand, the program must continue to address the personal and professional needs of new teachers as they join the faculty. At the same time, those teachers who have completed one year and are working on their professional development plans are at the beginning of a learning cycle that ideally will continue throughout their careers. These teachers still need time to collaborate and reflect about their practice as they continue to implement the activities outlined in their professional development plans. In that sense, the mentoring program continues beyond the scope of the one-year cycle we have described, and becomes an ongoing influence on the larger school community. To achieve this goal, the program committee, as well as the school administration and faculty, must focus on how the collaborative relationships that have been established can be extended after Year One, and on how this professional learning community can continue to provide guidance and support, not to new mentees only, but to all teachers.

So, where do you go from here? What happens next year? How do you accommodate the new mentees while you build on the work you have started? There are a number of strategies that address these questions and can sustain the momentum of the mentor program. These strategies include evaluating the past year's progress, safeguarding the time and other resources that have been devoted to the program, maintaining administrative support, and engaging the public. Ultimately, the faculty must use these resources along with its collective experience to craft and sustain a mentoring program that effectively supports both new teachers as well as those who are completing their professional development plans.

Evaluating the Past Year's Progress

The mentoring program must establish a learning cycle by evaluating feedback from the past year's activities and using the information to modify the program. We suggest that a steering committee be established, comprised of the mentor program coordinator, mentors, mentees, and administrators, to assist with the data analysis and to share anecdotal feedback. The committee can:

- Summarize the evaluations from the monthly seminars;
- Identify the areas of greatest teacher learning;
- Review the activities that most influenced classroom teaching;
- Evaluate pertinent student data;
- Use the suggestions that were offered to improve the monthly seminars.

Surveying the opinions of learning partners who completed the first year of the program can provide additional informative data. We have included a model survey at the end of this section. Based on this analysis the committee can make recommendations for program modifications and plan for the next year.

Time and Resources

In order to build upon the foundation you have built throughout the year, it is imperative to maintain the commitments of time, staffing, budget, and materials you have secured so far. We especially encourage you to preserve the established monthly support time. It has been our experience that when a designated time is purposely set and supported by teachers and administrators it becomes embedded into the school culture and recognized as a valuable part of the school organization.

Securing and maintaining the time and resources you need can be challenging. However, these issues can be resolved much more easily if the values and successes of the program are communicated to key stakeholders. We will touch on the importance of outreach communication later in this chapter.

New Teacher Support

Providing support and guidance for teachers new to the profession or new to the district remains at the core of the program. The process of establishing learning partnerships between new and experienced teachers – relationships that center on collaboration, reflective practice, a shared vision for professional growth, and a focus on student learning – continues to be the essential goal. While these basic components should remain unchanged, some program modifications may be required based on the analysis of the previous year's work.

Supporting Year Two Teachers: Completing the Professional Development Plan

Year One teachers progressed through a learning cycle centered on improved teaching practice and increased student learning in the context of a professional learning community. As a result, they identified learning goals based on reflection and analysis, and developed professional development plans to meet those goals. These professional development plans can only be implemented successfully in an environment that assigns them a high priority and supports their fulfillment. The monthly seminar can provide these teachers the time and space for continued collaboration, reflection, and support. At the same time, the expertise they have attained will be a valuable resource for new teachers and mentors during the seminars, especially when the focus in a particular month relates to the goals they are pursuing as part of their professional development plans.

Teachers in Year Two and beyond can also use the monthly seminars to:

- Collaborate with other teachers who are working on similar goals;
- Return to the list of resources listed in each month's chapters for assistance with further research;
- Complete additional activities that may help address the learning goals presented in the Professional Development Plan;
- Share dilemmas, struggles, and new insights with other teachers, and receive feedback and support from their colleagues.

Administrative Support

Principals and other administrative leaders must remain active participants in the mentor program to ensure its success. The following strategies present ways administrators can demonstrate and model support for the mentor program:

- Continue to attend monthly seminars;
- Be an active and knowledgeable participant in the monthly seminars, sharing your observations and other significant data with staff and community members;
- Share program results with other staff and community members when appropriate;
- Regard the learning partners as leaders in the school;
- Encourage other staff members to become part of the mentor program;
- Share the vision of the mentor program with staff and community;
- Be prepared to defend and promote program.

Public Engagement

If the mentor program is to be promoted and supported, all stakeholders must have an understanding of what the program is about and how it positively affects the school district. The following are strategies to communicate the value of the mentoring program.

Presentations to the School Board

We suggest that the program components be shared with the school board, together with personal stories from mentors and mentees and results that demonstrate the program's positive impact on teacher retention and student learning. Providing teachers a chance to share their professional development plans with board members, along with the data analysis and research that went into them, should provide a persuasive illustration that will help these key decision makers understand the methodology and relevance of the program.

Parent Support

Parents are often apprehensive when their child is placed in the classroom of a new teacher. Learning about the mentor program can reassure parents that the new teacher is receiving the guidance of a veteran teacher in a supportive learning community. Parents whose children have benefited from the program may be recruited to promote and support teacher mentoring. Details about the mentor program can be shared through school newsletters and at such events as Open House, Back to School Night, Parent/Teacher Conferences, and other school-sponsored activities.

Celebrate Successes

Celebrating the successful work of the learning partners is an important way to recognize and publicize the value of the mentor program. Recognition dinners, award ceremonies, receptions, and local newspaper coverage are possible ways to honor the mentor program publicly.

CONCLUSION

The mentor program presented in this book is designed to support mentors and mentees, as learning partners, to progress through the issues facing a teacher new to the profession, grade level, or district, and the challenges that confront all teachers. We based this program on the premise that all teachers need ongoing support and guidance of various kinds throughout their careers. We offer a sound program that assists mentee/mentor partners to benefit from a variety of learning experiences in a supportive environment based on standards of good teaching. The research-based concepts we present are beneficial not only for mentees and mentors, but are the components of any sound professional development program for educators.

Any successful organization must be an organization that promotes learning. A sound mentoring program is no different. The truly effective mentor program we envision builds the capacity of both new and veteran teachers to function in a professional learning community, with time to collaborate, reflect about teaching practice, and share a vision of good teaching, all focused on the ultimate goal of improved student learning. It is a community of learners where all teachers work not in isolation, but as collaborative partners or teams to discuss key issues, using real student work and real student data to improve teaching practice. It is an environment where instruction is grounded in a spirit of ongoing experimentation, observation, reflective inquiry, and dialogue.

We believe that the values expressed in this mentoring program extend far beyond the boundaries of the program itself, and can serve as a catalyst to help faculties transform the culture of their schools. The ultimate goal of our mentoring program, then, is to help all teachers discover a new and empowering vision of the teaching profession, one that will inspire them to work together to build continuous, sustained learning communities.

MONTH TEN

NEW TEACHER/MENTEE SURVEY

1. The biggest challenge I had this year was:

_____

_____

_____

_____

2. The most important thing I learned from my mentor was:

_____

_____

_____

_____

3. The most important things I learned from other colleagues in the mentor program were:

_____

_____

_____

_____

4. The monthly seminars I found most useful were (please check all that apply):

- ❑ Month One – Getting Acquainted
- ❑ Month Two – Current Reality
- ❑ Month Three – Analyzing Professional Practice and Standards
- ❑ Month Four – Analyzing Classroom Environment
- ❑ Month Five – Assessment
- ❑ Month Six – Content Standards and Curriculum
- ❑ Month Seven – Instructional Methods
- ❑ Month Eight –Setting Goals
- ❑ Month Nine – Writing the Professional Development Plan

Why were these seminars of particular value?

_____

_____

_____

5. The seminars I found least useful were (please check all that apply):

❏   Month One – Getting Acquainted
❏   Month Two – Current Reality
❏   Month Three – Analyzing Professional Practice and Standards
❏   Month Four – Analyzing Classroom Environment
❏   Month Five – Assessment
❏   Month Six – Content Standards and Curriculum
❏   Month Seven – Instructional Methods
❏   Month Eight –Setting Goals
❏   Month Nine – Writing the Professional Development Plan

Why were these seminars less useful?

_____
_____
_____

6. I would change the monthly support seminars in these ways:

_____
_____
_____

7. How did keeping a reflection journal help me focus on student learning?

_____
_____
_____

8. How did keeping a reflection journal help me become a more effective teacher?

_____
_____
_____

9. One thing I wish we had discussed during the monthly seminars was:

_____
_____
_____

MONTH TEN

10. The advice I would give to the coordinator of the mentor program is:

_____

_____

_____

11. Am I interested in continuing the relationship I have with my learning partner?

_____

If yes, what do I need to continue this relationship?

_____

12. Overall how would I rate my relationship with my learning partner?

1	2	3	4	5	6
not helpful					extremely helpful

Comments: _____

_____

_____

13. How would I rate the overall effectiveness of the mentor program?

1	2	3	4	5	6
not helpful					extremely helpful

Comments: _____

_____

_____

MENTOR SURVEY

1. The biggest challenge that I had this year as a mentor was:

_____

_____

_____

2. If I were to give advice to a new mentor, it would be:

_____

_____

_____

3. The most important things I learned from my mentee was:

_____

_____

_____

4. The most important things I learned from other colleagues in the mentor program were:

_____

_____

_____

5. The monthly seminars I found most useful were (please check all that apply):

❑ Month One – Getting Acquainted
❑ Month Two – Current Reality
❑ Month Three – Analyzing Professional Practice and Standards
❑ Month Four – Analyzing Classroom Environment
❑ Month Five – Assessment
❑ Month Six – Content Standards and Curriculum
❑ Month Seven – Instructional Methods
❑ Month Eight – Setting Goals
❑ Month Nine – Writing the Professional Development Plan

Why were these seminars of particular value?

_____

_____

_____

MONTH TEN

6. The seminars I found least useful were (please check all that apply):

❑   Month One – Getting Acquainted
❑   Month Two – Current Reality
❑   Month Three – Analyzing Professional Practice and Standards
❑   Month Four – Analyzing Classroom Environment
❑   Month Five – Assessment
❑   Month Six – Content Standards and Curriculum
❑   Month Seven – Instructional Methods
❑   Month Eight – Setting Goals
❑   Month Nine – Writing the Professional Development Plan

Why were these seminars less useful?

_____
_____
_____

7. I would change the monthly support seminars in these ways:

_____
_____
_____

8. One thing I wish we had discussed during the monthly seminars was:

_____
_____
_____

9. How did keeping a reflection journal help me focus on student learning?

_____
_____
_____

10. How did keeping a reflection journal help me become a more effective teacher?

_____

_____

_____

11. The advice I'd give to the program coordinator is:

_____

_____

_____

12. Am I interested in continuing the relationship I have with my learning partner?

_____

_____

_____

If yes, what do I need to continue this relationship?

_____

_____

_____

13. How would I rate my relationship with my learning partner?

1	2	3	4	5	6
not helpful					extremely helpful

Comments: _____

_____

_____

14. How would I rate the overall effectiveness of the mentor program?

1	2	3	4	5	6
not helpful					extremely helpful

Comments: _____

_____

Appendix

A. MONTHLY MENTEE/MENTOR CHECKLISTS
B. MONTHLY ADMINISTRATOR CHECKLISTS
C. MONTHLY COORDINATOR CHECKLIST

APPENDIX A
MONTHLY MENTEE/MENTOR CHECKLISTS

The following checklists are designed to help new teachers research specific details related to school operations, and to be aware of seasonal occurrences throughout the year that impact teaching and learning. Mentees should discuss these with their mentor partners.

Before School Starts (This will vary for year-round schools)

Supplies: ❏ Where supplies are stored ❏ What supplies are available	**Parking:** ❏ Parking lot location ❏ Parking policies
Resources and Equipment: ❏ Audio-visual equipment location and check-out ❏ Audio-visual equipment instruction ❏ Copy machine location ❏ Copy machine policies and instruction ❏ Copy center requests ❏ Resource center procedures	**Schedules:** ❏ School schedule ❏ Computer lab schedule ❏ Special classes schedules ❏ Student lunch schedules ❏ Teacher lunch schedules ❏ School calendar and key events ❏ School in-service days, late starts, early release ❏ School programs ❏ School board meetings
Tours: ❏ Building ❏ Community	**Goals:** ❏ Building ❏ District
Emergency Procedures: ❏ Fire drill ❏ Tornado drill ❏ Bomb threat ❏ School shooting ❏ Lock-down drill	**Discipline Policies:** ❏ Classroom ❏ Playground ❏ Lunch room ❏ School property ❏ Bus ❏ Office referrals
Staff: ❏ Staff introductions ❏ List of staff and phone numbers ❏ Specialists and their roles ❏ Administrators and their roles ❏ Other district/building personnel ❏ Teacher aide availability ❏ Building maintenance	**Non-Instructional Duties:** ❏ Hall duty ❏ Recess ❏ Before school ❏ Lunch room ❏ Extra-curricular activities ❏ Chaperoning school events
Attendance Policies: ❏ Teacher sick day procedures ❏ Preparing substitute folder ❏ Teacher personal day procedures ❏ Substitute request policy ❏ Teachers leaving school during the day policies and procedures ❏ Student attendance procedures and record keeping ❏ School cancellation procedures	**Record Keeping:** ❏ Lesson plan procedures ❏ Organizing a grade book ❏ Cumulative folders ❏ Student information cards **In-service and Faculty Meetings:** ❏ Expectations for faculty meetings ❏ In-service options and requirements
Lunch: ❏ Lunch routine – students ❏ Lunch ticket procedures ❏ Lunch money procedures	**Parent Communication:** ❏ Parent communication policies ❏ Parent orientation information ❏ Home visit procedures and policies
School Visitors: ❏ School visitor policies and procedures ❏ School volunteers policies and procedures ❏ Guidelines for bringing in guest speakers	**Pay Procedures:** ❏ Pay periods ❏ Salary classification ❏ Extended contract policies
❏ In-school Phone Usage	❏ Bus Procedures
❏ Safe Keeping of Valuables	❏ District Demographic Information
Union: ❏ School representative ❏ Grievance procedure ❏ Copy of negotiated agreement	**Standing Committees:** ❏ Curriculum ❏ Social ❏ Other
❏ Playground Rules/Equipment	❏ Supervision/Evaluation Policies and Procedures

Other Comments/Suggestions/Helpful Hints:

MONTHLY MENTEE/MENTOR CHECKLISTS

September/October

Parent Communication: ❑ Back to School Night ❑ Open House ❑ Orientations	**Curriculum:** ❑ Review existing curriculum ❑ Curriculum planning and expectations
Parent Teacher Conferences: ❑ Ready-set-goal conferences ❑ Parent teacher conference policies ❑ Who schedules ❑ Length of time ❑ What is shared ❑ Student participation	**Student Information:** ❑ Students who are in transitional housing ❑ Students who live in shelters ❑ Students who are bussed ❑ Students who are in after-school daycare ❑ Student who begin school after the scheduled start date ❑ Student medication ❑ Student health concerns
❑ Professional Development Opportunities	
❑ Extra Curricular School Activities/Duties/Responsibilities	❑ Work Orders/Maintenance
❑ Classroom and/or Course Change Procedure	❑ Special Ed. Referral Procedure
❑ Parent Organizations (PTO)	❑ Grade Level/Department Meetings
❑ Homework Policies	❑ School Related Clubs/Programs
❑ In-service Days	❑ 504 IEP Procedures
Assessment Issues: ❑ Progress reports ❑ Review Report Card ❑ Specific quarter reports (specific to grade level and program) ❑ District-wide testing program ❑ State-wide testing program	❑ Student and Staff Birthday Procedures and Policies
	❑ Youth Tutoring Program
	❑ Homebound Student Policy
Portfolio Procedures: ❑ What is included ❑ Storage ❑ What is the format (i.e., electronic)	❑ Remediation Program
	Teacher Evaluation: ❑ Procedures and policies ❑ Quarterly meeting with principal to discuss formal evaluation procedures
Field Trip Policies: ❑ Chaperones ❑ Permission slip policies ❑ Procedure for money collection ❑ Policy for students who are unable to pay ❑ Emergency contact policy	**All-School Assemblies:** ❑ Cultural arts programs ❑ All-school music programs ❑ Concerts ❑ Pep rallies ❑ Other
Classroom Party Policies: ❑ Students with food allergies ❑ Room parents ❑ Planning	**Classroom Volunteer Procedures/Policies:** ❑ Parents ❑ College students ❑ Senior citizens ❑ Other
❑ Halloween Party Policy and Procedure	❑ Homecoming Festivities

Other Comments/Suggestions/Helpful Hints:

MONTHLY MENTEE/MENTOR CHECKLISTS

November/December

❑ Weather Related School Cancellation Procedure
❑ Review School Cancellation Procedures
❑ Budget Requests

District Winter Holiday Activities/Policies:
    ❑ Gift giving policies
    ❑ Gift receiving policies
    ❑ Decorations
    ❑ Classroom parties
    ❑ Music programs
    ❑ Staff party
    ❑ Student all-school party/dance

Winter Sports:
    ❑ Faculty responsibility
    ❑ Schedule

❑ Flu Shot
❑ Importance of Accurate Enrollment Counts
❑ Observation and Feedback

Other Comments/Suggestions/Helpful Hints:

MONTHLY MENTEE/MENTOR CHECKLISTS

January/February

❑ End of the Semester Procedures
❑ Report Cards/Records Days
❑ Strategies to Get Through the Winter
❑ Final Semester Grading
❑ Retention Policies
❑ Secondary School Scheduling
❑ Plan for Second Semester
❑ Quarterly Meeting with Principal (January)
❑ Student and Teacher Illness
❑ Student Make-Up Work Policy

Grading Policies:
    ❑ Incomplete grades
    ❑ Changing grades

Standardized Testing Issues/Policies:
    ❑ Scheduling
    ❑ What grade levels are assessed
    ❑ District
    ❑ State
    ❑ Procedure for collecting tests

❑ Begin Talking About Summer and/or Next Year Staff Development Opportunities
❑ Contract Renewal/Nonrenewal

Valentine's Day:
    ❑ Parties
    ❑ School activities

❑ Winter Dance
❑ Planning Spring Programs/Trips
❑ Observation and Feedback

Other Comments/Suggestions/Helpful Hints:

MONTHLY MENTEE/MENTOR CHECKLISTS

March

❑	Review Diagnostic Testing Procedures
❑	Contract Signing
❑	Year-End Reports
❑	Transfer Policies
❑	Special Ed. Year-End State Reporting
❑	Review IEP Procedures
❑	Fall Ordering Films/Kits
❑	Quarterly Meeting with Principal (March and June)
❑	Additional Records Aside from Cum. Folders
❑	Student Awards Policy
❑	Spring Break
❑	Student Absence Due to Family Vacation
❑	Winter Sports Tournaments

Other Comments/Suggestions/Helpful Hints:

MONTHLY MENTEE/MENTOR CHECKLISTS

April/May/June

☐ Review Diagnostic Testing Procedures
☐ Daylight Savings Time
☐ Year-End Activities/Awards
☐ Kindergarten Registration/Orientation for Fall Kindergarten Students
☐ Year-End Cum. Folder Information
☐ Summer School Referrals
☐ Portfolio Transfers Policies & Procedures
☐ Scheduling for Next Year
☐ Class Lists for Next Year
☐ Budgeting for Next Year
☐ Scholarship Procedures
☐ Last Day Check Out Procedures
☐ Support for Stresses of Last 2 Weeks of School – Impact on Professional and Personal Life

Graduation and/or Promotion Activities and Policies:
    ☐ Dates
    ☐ Informal/formal
    ☐ Celebration policies

End-of-Year Clean-Up and Storage Policies:
    ☐ Classroom inventories
    ☐ Labeling stored items
    ☐ Storage – how and where

Spring/Year-End Activities:
    ☐ Prom
    ☐ Picnics
    ☐ Field trips
    ☐ Concerts
    ☐ Banquets
    ☐ Awards programs

☐ CELEBRATE

Other Comments/Suggestions/Helpful Hints:

APPENDIX B
MONTHLY ADMINISTRATOR CHECKLISTS

The following lists outline specific tasks to be completed by the building administrator to help implement and support the mentor program.

MONTH ONE
Getting Acquainted

- ❏ Attend monthly seminar
- ❏ Assist Coordinator with seminar organization as needed
- ❏ Openly support the value of the mentor program at staff meetings and in other school communications
- ❏ Welcome all mentors and mentees
- ❏ Explain your role in the mentor program
- ❏ Describe how you will be available for support
- ❏ Assure mentors and mentees that the content of their discussions is confidential

---

MONTH TWO
Current Reality

- ❏ Attend monthly seminar
- ❏ Assist Coordinator with seminar organization as needed
- ❏ Openly support the value of the mentor program at staff meetings and in other school communications
- ❏ Provide district parent-teacher conference policies
- ❏ Modify classroom schedules to accommodate mentee and mentor to investigate district/building data

Provide:
- ❏ Demographic data about the district

MONTHLY ADMINISTRATOR CHECKLISTS

MONTH THREE
Analyzing Professional Practice

❑ Attend monthly seminar
❑ Assist Coordinator with seminar organization as needed
❑ Openly support the value of the mentor program at staff meetings and other school communications
❑ Share knowledge of teaching standards and rubrics
❑ Explain evaluation policies and procedures
❑ Provide opportunities for staff development
❑ Explain classroom observation policies:
  • Formal
  • Informal

MONTH FOUR
Analyzing Classroom Environment

❑ Attend monthly seminar
❑ Assist Coordinator with seminar organization as needed
❑ Openly support the value of the mentor program at staff meetings and other school communications
Provide any school climate data:
❑ Disciplinary procedures and policies
❑ Climate study results

MONTHLY ADMINISTRATOR CHECKLISTS

MONTH FIVE
Assessment

❏ Attend monthly seminar
❏ Assist Coordinator with seminar organization as needed
❏ Openly support the value of the mentor program at staff meetings and other school communications
❏ Explain the security procedures regarding standardized testing
❏ Provide district standardized test data to mentees and mentors
❏ Explain the procedure for collecting, analyzing, and disseminating the standardized test data
❏ Explain how the standardized test results are used in the district
❏ Explain how the standardized test results are communicated to the public
❏ Provide any building or district assessments

MONTH SIX
Content Standards and Curriculum

❏ Attend monthly seminar
❏ Assist Coordinator with seminar organization as needed
❏ Openly support the value of the mentor program at staff meetings and other school communications
❏ Provide copies of the state and local content standards
❏ Prominently display content standards in building
❏ Provide building and district curriculum guides to mentees and mentors

MONTHLY ADMINISTRATOR CHECKLISTS

MONTH SEVEN
Instructional Methods

- ❑ Attend monthly support seminar
- ❑ Assist Coordinator with seminar organization as needed
- ❑ Openly support the value of the mentor program at staff meetings and other school communications
- ❑ Modify classroom schedules to accommodate mentee and mentor classroom visits
- ❑ Encourage classroom visits
- ❑ Assure mentors and mentees that their classroom visits are not evaluations
- ❑ Assure mentors and mentees that the content of the classroom visits are confidential

---

MONTH EIGHT
Setting Goals

- ❑ Attend monthly support seminar
- ❑ Assist Coordinator with seminar organization as needed
- ❑ Openly support the value of the mentor program at staff meetings and other school communications

MONTHLY ADMINISTRATOR CHECKLISTS

MONTH NINE
Writing the Professional Development Plan

- ❑ Attend monthly support seminar
- ❑ Assist Coordinator with seminar organization as needed
- ❑ Openly support the value of the mentor program at staff meetings and other school communications
- ❑ Offer assistance to learning partners as they develop their professional development plans. This assistance could include:
  - Offering staff development opportunities
  - Schedule modifications
  - Classroom visits
  - Offering resources

MONTH TEN AND BEYOND
The Cycle Continues

- ❑ Be part of the steering committee that evaluates and modifies mentor program
- ❑ Assist in planning for the following year
- ❑ Assist with scheduling to keep the mentor program monthly seminar time sacred
- ❑ Present mentor program analysis to school board
- ❑ Encourage other teachers to become involved in the mentor program
- ❑ Be part of the year-end celebration

APPENDIX C
MONTHLY COORDINATOR CHECKLIST

The following chart will assist the coordinator with the responsibilities of organizing the monthly support seminars. Check the appropriate box as each task is completed. The last row lists tasks specific to the topic of the monthly seminar.

	Month One	Month Two	Month Three	Month Four	Month Five
Set meeting time and place					
Communicate meeting time and place to all participants					
Send reminders to all participants					
Disseminate feedback forms 2-3 weeks prior to seminar					
Collect feedback forms – one week prior to seminar					
Review feedback forms and set agenda					
Review agenda with building administrator					
Arrange for refreshments					
Arrange room					
Photocopy agenda and evaluation forms					
Set up refreshments					
Specific monthly responsibilities	❑ Provide district demographic data	❑ Provide state standards and rubrics for teaching (if available) ❑ Provide professional practice resources	❑ Provide classroom management resources	❑ Provide district assessment information ❑ Provide assessment resources	

MONTHLY COORDINATOR CHECKLIST

	Month Six	Month Seven	Month Eight	Month Nine	Months Ten-Twelve
Set meeting time and place					For steering committee
Communicate meeting time and place to all participants					For steering committee
Send reminders to all participants					For steering committee
Disseminate feedback forms 2-3 weeks prior to seminar					Not applicable
Collect feedback forms – one week prior to seminar					Not applicable
Review feedback forms and set agenda					Not applicable
Review agenda with building administrator					Not applicable
Arrange for refreshments					For celebration
Arrange room					For celebration
Photocopy agenda and evaluation forms					Not applicable
Set up refreshments					For celebration
Specific monthly responsibilities	❑ Provide district curriculum guides ❑ Provide state and local standards ❑ Provide curriculum and standards resources	❑ Provide instructional methodologies resources			❑ Organize and facilitate steering committee changes ❑ Plan end of year celebration ❑ Plan school board presentation ❑ Plan for next year ❑ Collect all data sources: ❑ Monthly seminar evaluations ❑ Mentor and mentee surveys ❑ Anecdotal data

INDEX

continued reflection and, 178
courses, 58
goals, xxvii, 2, 15, 175
job-embedded, xi
opportunities, 205
shared vision for ongoing/job-embedded, xi, xv, xvi-
    xvii
Professional development/growth plan, xviii, xxi, xxvi,
    xxix, 158, 159, 164, 165, 166, 174, 178, 192, 194
"action steps," 175-176
completing, 193-194
components, xxi
"current status," 175
evidence, 177
evidence summary, 177
format, 175
goals, xxi
"goal statement," 175
implementation, xxi
manageable, 174, 175
meaningful, 174, 175
measurable, 174, 175
plan of action, xxi
questions to answer, 174
resources needed, 176
revisions, 177, 182, 184
targeting goals, 60
timelines, xxi, 176-177
    See also Professional development plan, writing
Professional development plan, writing, xxi, 174-178,
    179, 180-185, 186-190, 196, 197, 199, 200, 214.
        See also Month nine (writing professional devel-
        opment plan)
Professional development plan format, 175
Professional learning community, viii, x, xi, xv, xvii,
    xxvi, xxxv, 39, 192, 193, 195
collaborative, xxvi
creating, xiv
focus, xvii
mentor/mentee partnerships in, xv
school culture, x
teacher unions and, xxxiii
    See also Learning community
Professional learning community literature, xi
Professional practice, analyzing, xix, 38-39, 40, 41-50,
    51-55. See also Month three (analyzing profes-
    sional practice)
Professional standards. See Standards, professional
Public engagement, 194

Reeves, D., 86, 130

Reflection, ix, xiv, xvi, xvii, xviii, 2, 3, 14, 39, 58, 60,
    140, 174, 178, 185, 193
art of, xvi
fostering continuous, xvi
promoting, xiv
    See also Group reflection; Monthly Reflection
        Journal Summary; Self-reflection; Weekly
        Teacher Reflection Journal
Reflective dialogue, thoughtful, xvi
Reflective practice, xi, xv, xvi
Reflective practitioner, ix
Reflective process, xix. See also Month one (introducing
    mentoring partners to reflective process)
Reflective thinking, xxvi
culture of, xvi
Regulations:
district, 20
Relationships, xiii
classroom, 75
collaborative, 192
mentoring, xxxv
new/experienced teacher, 193
peer, 75
reciprocal, xiv
social, 76
successful mentoring, xxx
working, 6
    See also Mentor/mentee relationship
Resources, xviii, xix, xxiii, xxvi, xxx, 2, 20, 21, 23, 28,
    29, 30, 39, 43, 44, 45, 46, 47, 49, 59, 60, 69, 75,
    129, 143, 146, 147, 159, 164, 165, 174, 176, 180,
    182, 184, 192, 193, 194, 204, 214, 215, 216
month eight, 160
month five, 88
month four, 62-65
month nine, 179
month one, 4
month seven, 144
month six, 125
month three, 40
month two, 22
Respect, xi, xv, 1, 3, 59, 72, 73, 76, 142
Responsibility, shared, 2, 59, 69, 70, 76
Revisions, professional development plan, 177, 182, 184
Rubrics, viii, 89, 90, 93, 100, 106, 107-110, 177, 181
Rules, 7, 8, 20, 28, 29, 47, 69, 70, 72, 181, 204

Sargent, J., 141
School board, 100, 214, 216
    presentations to, 194
School board meetings, 204

**CORWIN
PRESS**

The Corwin Press logo—a raven striding across an open book—represents the happy union of courage and learning. We are a professional-level publisher of books and journals for K-12 educators, and we are committed to creating and providing resources that embody these qualities. Corwin's motto is "Success for All Learners."